CoolBrands® 2014/15
An insight into some of Britain's coolest brands

Credits

2014/15
CoolBrands.uk.com

03

Chief Executive
Ben Hudson

Managing Editor
Rebecca Perry

Brand Liaison Directors
Liz Silvester
Daren Thomas

Brand Liaison Manager
Amanda Gilbert

Designer
Ami Sunners

Proofreader
Angela Cooper

Head of Accounts
Will Carnochan

Published by
Superbrands (UK) Ltd
22-23 Little Portland Street
London
W1W 8BU

Colour reproduction by
Pixel Colour Imaging

Printed in Italy

ISBN: 978-0-9565334-8-7

All rights reserved.

© 2014 Superbrands (UK) Ltd
CoolBrands® is a registered trademark of Superbrands (UK) Ltd in the United Kingdom.

No part of this publication may be reproduced or transmitted in any form by any means, electronic, digital or mechanical, including scanning, photocopying, recording or any information storage and retrieval system relating to all or part of the text, photographs, logotypes without first obtaining permission in writing from the publisher of the book together with the copyright owners as featured.

MIX
Paper from responsible sources
FSC
www.fsc.org
FSC® C015829

Foreword

CoolBrands® asked Jamal Edwards, Digital Entrepreneur and Founder of SB.TV, what cool means to him…

As a young boy I always used to think about what made something cool. Was it because it was attractive, trendy, different or unique? I think, now, I have finally figured out what it means – the 'cool' we often search for is the thing that makes us individual, at the same time as being part of a collective. Cool is a state of mind, a way of living, a way of being. To be cool is not necessarily to be famous or popular but is more to do with the way you define the world around you through the ideologies you attach yourself to.

In my opinion, to be cool is not to define your identity against a product. I exist in the era of the digital influencer; for us, 'cool' arrived in the form of opportunistic innovation, but it doesn't stop there.

Cool is the trend before it is given a name, the feeling of getting closer to defining the 'you', the idea before the physical embodiment. The notion of self, for me, is the lifeblood of what is to be cool. The more confident your feel about yourself, the cooler those around you perceive you to be; a cool life is one about being true to yourself.

Jamal Edwards
Digital Entrepreneur & Founder, SB.TV
CoolBrands® Expert Council member

Contents

08	About CoolBrands®		Destinology
10	Who chooses the CoolBrands®?		first direct
			Fred & Ginger
	1936 Bière		**Gaucho**
	Adnams		**ghd**
	Alexander McQueen		**Graham & Brown**
	Alternative Flooring		**Green & Black's Organic**
	Apple		**GYMBOX**
	Aspall Cyder		**Heal's**
	Aveda		**Home House**
	Balthazar		**Hotel Café Royal**
	Bisque		**Hotel du Vin**
	Bolin Webb		**HouseTrip**
	Cambridge Audio		**itsu**
	Chapel Down		**JO LOVES**
	Charlotte Olympia		**Kopparberg**
	Courvoisier		**Krispy Kreme**
	Crussh		**Laurent-Perrier**
	Daylesford		**Lavazza**
	Dermalogica		**Linda Farrow**

2014/15
CoolBrands.uk.com

07

Malmaison	Tangle Teezer
McLaren Automotive	The French Bedroom Company
ME London	The House of St Barnabas
Mercedes-Benz	The May Fair
Mövenpick Ice Cream	The O2
NARS	The Saucy Fish Co.
No.1 Lounges	The Zetter Townhouse
Pedlars	TONI&GUY
Philip Kingsley	Trinity Leeds
Pret A Manger	Tunetribe
Rapha	Urbanears
Rekorderlig	Virgin Atlantic
Rockett St George	Virgin Money
Salty Dog	
Sipsmith	152 Expert Council 2014/15
Sonos	166 Qualifying CoolBrands® 2014/15
Sony Music	
Spotify	
Stella McCartney	
Storm	

About CoolBrands®

2014/15
CoolBrands.uk.com

09

CoolBrands® is an annual initiative to identify and pay tribute to the nation's coolest brands.

Since 2001 we have been canvassing the opinions of experts and consumers to produce an annual barometer of Britain's coolest brands, people and places.

Cool is subjective and personal. Accordingly, voters are not given a definition but are asked to bear in mind the following factors, which research has shown are inherent in all CoolBrands®…

Style
Originality
Desirability

Innovation
Authenticity
Uniqueness

Brands do not apply or pay to be considered for CoolBrands® status.

Who chooses the CoolBrands®?

2014/15
CoolBrands.uk.com

The 2014/15 CoolBrands® were chosen by an Expert Council and thousands of members of the British public. The entire selection process is independently administered by The Centre for Brand Analysis – visit CoolBrands.uk.com for full details.

11

The 2014/15 Expert Council

Stephen Cheliotis	Chief Executive, The Centre for Brand Analysis (TCBA) & Chairman, CoolBrands® Expert Council
Bip Ling	Blogger, DJ & Model
Carl Barât	Musician & Actor
Charli XCX	Singer
Charlotte Riley	Actress
David Harewood MBE	Actor
Eleanor Tomlinson	Actress
Ella Eyre	Singer-Songwriter
Emily Hartridge	International YouTuber & Presenter
Emily Johnston	Blogger
Gisèle Scanlon	Writer, Broadcaster, Artist & Co-Founder, the goddessguide.com
Izzy Lawrence	DJ, TV Presenter & Blogger
Jamal Edwards	Digital Entrepreneur & Founder, SB.TV
James-lee Duffy	Art Director & Illustrator, We Are Shadows
Jodie Kidd	International Model
Jonathan Bailey	Actor
Julien Macdonald OBE	Fashion Designer
Justin Wilkes	DJ, Kisstory/Kiss FM UK
Kate Halfpenny	Fashion Designer & Stylist
Kelly Hoppen MBE	Designer, Author & Entrepreneur
Labrinth	Singer-Songwriter
Laura Jackson	TV Presenter
Laura Mvula	Singer-Songwriter
Liz Matthews	Publicist
Mark Krendel	Managing Director, 8lbs
Melissa Odabash	Fashion Designer
Millie Kendall MBE	Beauty Brand Creator
Natasha McNamara	Digital Editor, glamour.com
Phil Clifton	XFM DJ & Presenter
Reverend and The Makers	Indie-Pop Band
Ruby Hammer MBE	Make-Up Artist
Sadie Frost	Actress & Fashion Designer
Sam Hall (Goldierocks)	International DJ & Broadcaster
Sophie Dahl	International Model & Writer
Spark	Singer-Songwriter
Susan Riley	Deputy Editor, Stylist Magazine
Tom Findlay	DJ & Producer
Will Best	TV Presenter

Turn to page 152 for more about the Expert Council

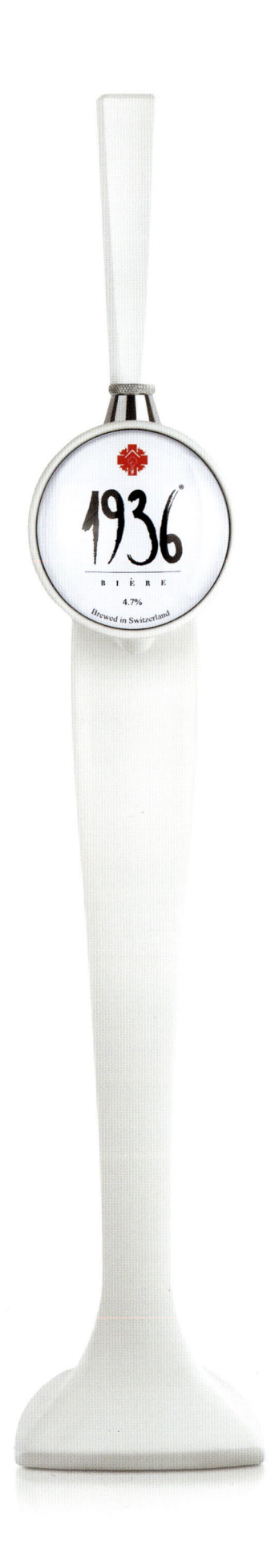

1936
BIÈRE
4.7%
Brewed in Switzerland

1936 Bière

Brewed by the Locher family at the foot of the Swiss Alps using only the purest water, 1936 Bière has a unique, fresh and ultra clean taste.

The water used to brew 1936 Bière filters through the Swiss Alps, taking up to 25 years to reach the source. This unique water is combined with raw ingredients – Swiss hops and golden barley grown at high altitude on the mountains – to create a beer totally free from artificial preservatives or additives. Long famous for its innovative prowess in the development of new beers, the 1936 Bière brewery also leads in the field of climate protection.

1936biere.com

Some of the fresh Southwold air we put into all of our beers

ADNAMS.
SOUTHWOLD

Stray piece of air from inland, we'd never use it

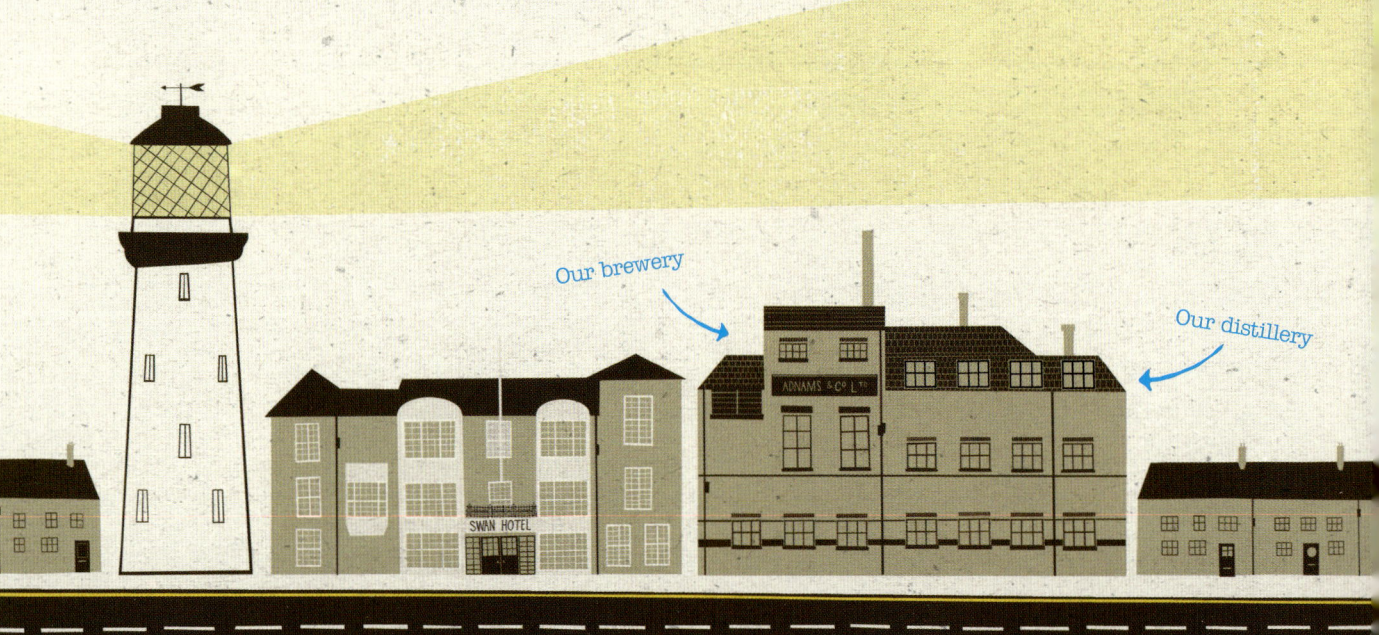

Our brewery

Our distillery

Get to know us a bit better at adnams.co.uk

2014/15
CoolBrands.uk.com

Adnams

Based in sunny Southwold, with a range of award-winning beers and craft spirits, Adnams is a company that prides itself on doing things differently.

Founded in 1872, with a passion for quality and an instinct for innovation, Adnams can be found throughout East Anglia and London today. From local grains to exotic hops and botanicals Fergus, the brewer, and John, the distiller, use a wide range of ingredients to create tasty beers and spirits. At home in trendy craft beer bars, stylish restaurants and cosy pubs, Adnams works hard to ensure its impact on its community and the environment is a positive one.

ADNAMS
SOUTHWOLD

adnams.co.uk

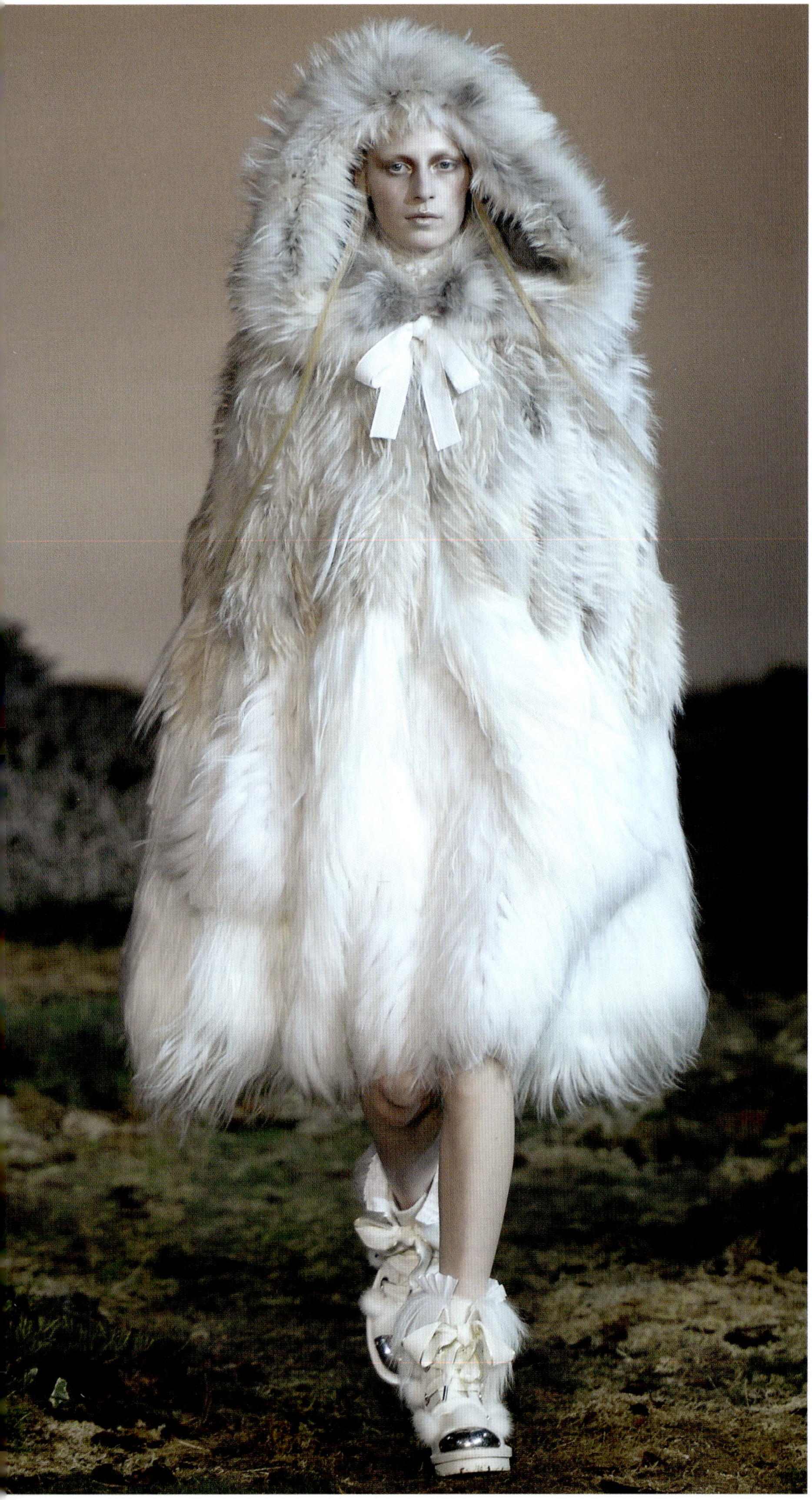
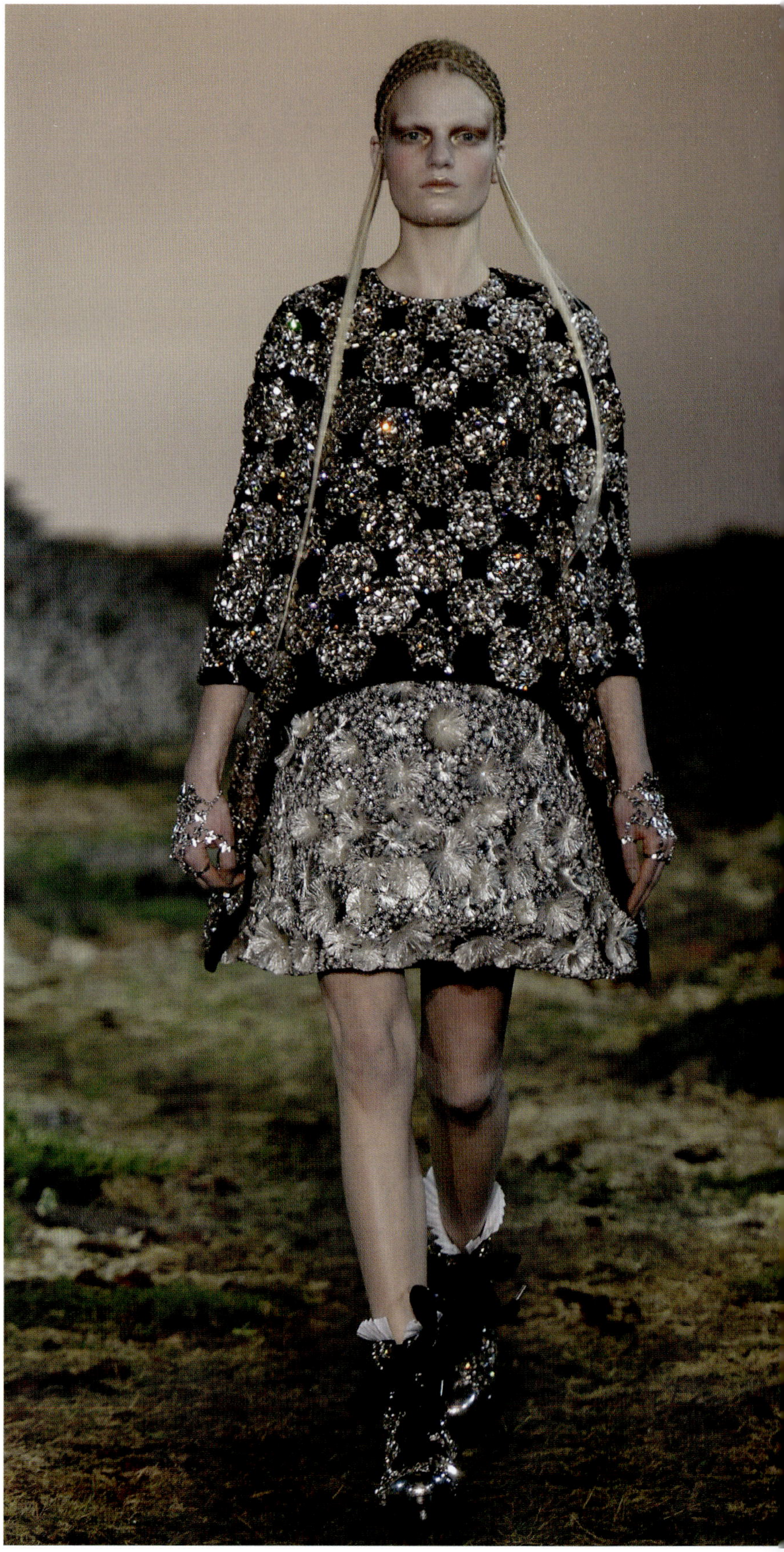

2014/15
CoolBrands.uk.com

Alexander McQueen

A mix of razor sharp tailoring, the fine workmanship of the haute couture atelier and impeccable manufacturing creates the signature Alexander McQueen look.

Known for the juxtaposition of contrasting elements – fragility and strength, tradition and modernity, fluidity and severity – the brand is influenced by the arts and crafts tradition, for which it has profound respect. Famed for the emotional power and energy of its shows as well as the romantic but contemporary nature of its collections, Sarah Burton, Creative Director, continues the Alexander McQueen legacy. Her critically acclaimed collections fuse the McQueen aesthetic with her signature handcraft and technical expertise.

ALEXANDER McQUEEN

alexandermcqueen.com

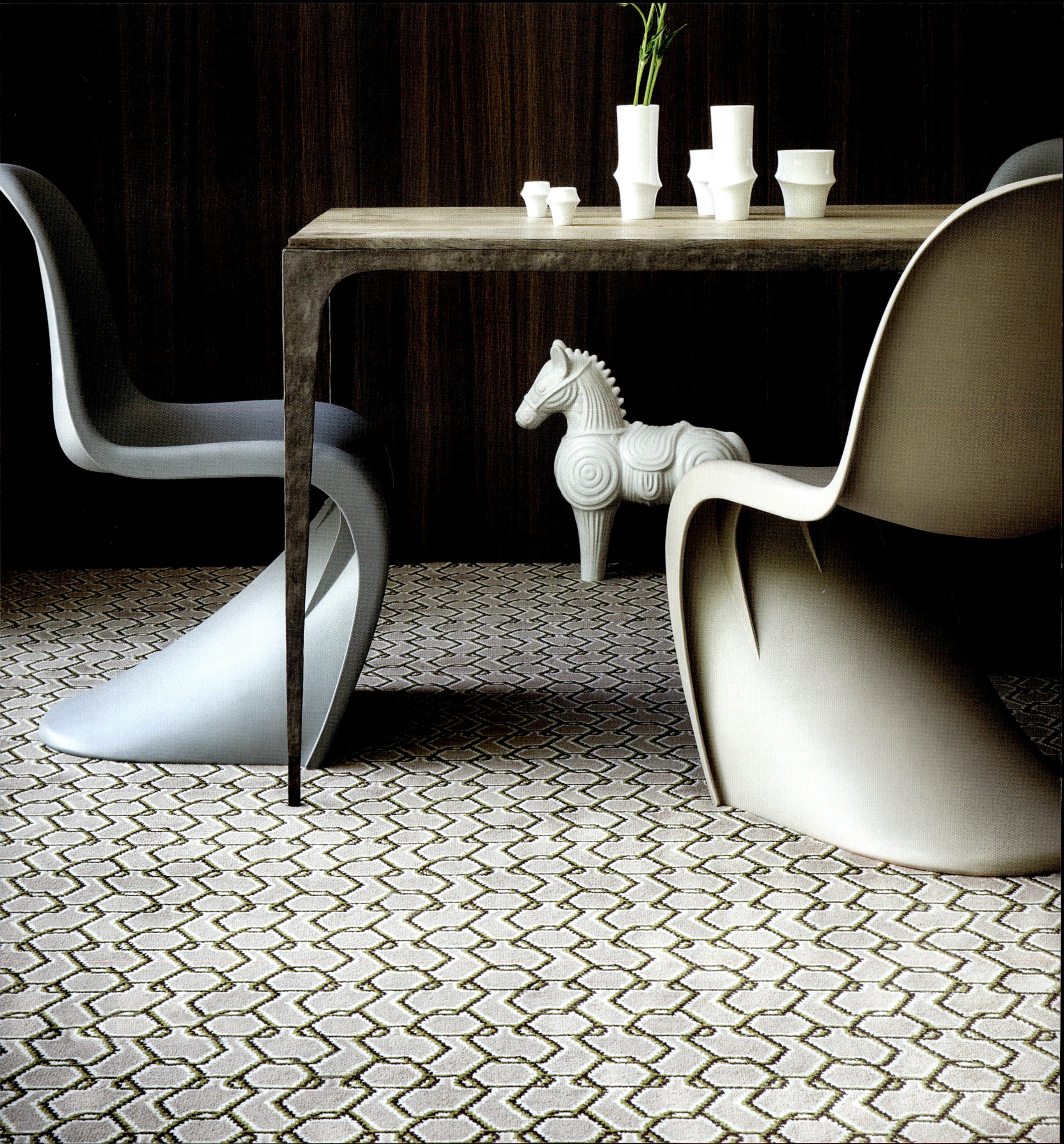

2014/15
CoolBrands.uk.com

Alternative Flooring

With a spark of curiosity that inspires flooring to be different, Alternative Flooring is an award-winning brand that embraces a creative spirit and unconventional thinking.

With a modern mix of carpet, rugs and runners that is big on natural texture and packed with colour, Alternative Flooring is changing how people look and feel about floors. The brand is refashioning floors with carpets which are classic yet forward-looking. Quirky B, a patterned carpet collection which includes collaborations with British designers Ashley Hicks and Margo Selby, hits just the right notes to make carpet sing again.

alternative flooring

alternativeflooring.com

iPad
9:41 AM
100%
Tuesday
22
FaceTime
Calendar
Photos
Camera
Contacts
Clock
Maps
Videos
Notes
Reminders
Photo Booth
Game Center
Newsstand
iTunes Store
App Store
Settings
Messages
Mail
Safari
Music
iPad

2014/15
CoolBrands.uk.com

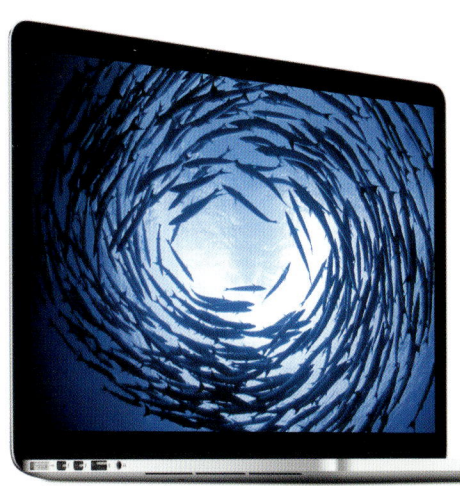

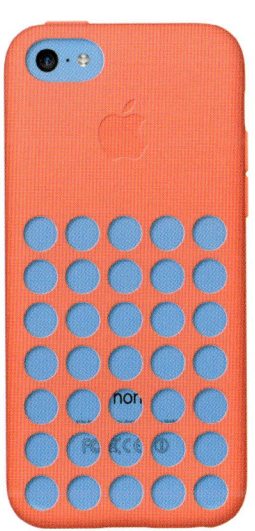

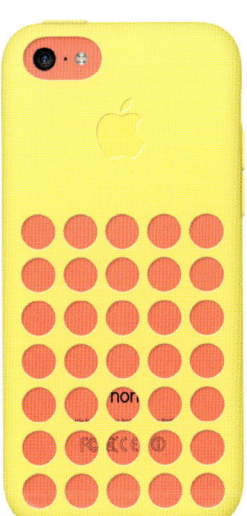

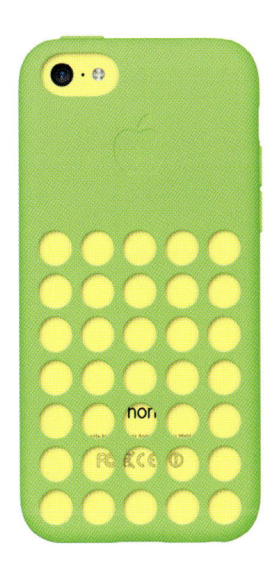

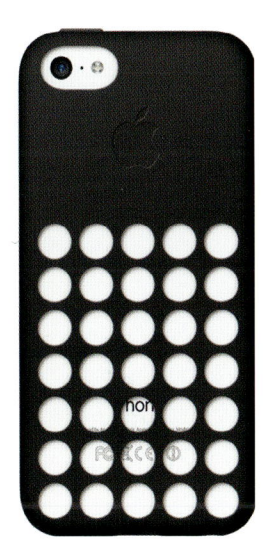

Apple

Sleek, stylish design combined with powerful, groundbreaking technology make Apple's range of products iconic must-haves around the world.

Apple ignited the personal computer revolution in the 1970s with Apple II and reinvented the personal computer in the 1980s with the Macintosh. Continuing to lead the industry with its award-winning computers, Apple has spearheaded the digital media revolution. Apple reinvented the mobile phone with its iPhone and App Store, and remains at the cutting edge of technology, recently launching an iPad with retina display, the thinnest, lightest iPod touch and the fastest ever MacBook Air.

apple.com

ESTD 1728
ASPALL
HARRY SPARROW
SUFFOLK CYDER
CRAFTED IN SUFFOLK - ALC. 4.6% VOL.
ESTD 1728
ASPALL
SUFFOLK
DRAUGHT CYDER
CRAFTED IN SUFFOLK - ALC. 5.5% VOL.
ESTD 1728
ASPALL
IMPERIAL VINTAGE №285
SUFFOLK CYDER
CRAFTED IN SUFFOLK - ALC. 8.2% VOL.

2014/15
CoolBrands.uk.com

Aspall Cyder

The Chevalliers began crafting cyder at Aspall, Suffolk in 1728. Eight generations on they remain obsessed with creating the finest products from the best fruit.

Barry and Henry Chevallier are proud custodians of the legacy of Clement, a Huguenot refugee who chose a very special corner of England for his ancestral home, Aspall Hall. The Chevallier family still lives there, among Clement's Suffolk orchards, which blossom in spring and reap their annual autumnal rewards. Apples pressed on site produce the very finest, world-class cyders and cyder vinegars – emblems of the modern artisans, enjoying increasingly global acclaim for quality and excellence.

ESTD 1728
ASPALL
SUFFOLK

aspall.co.uk

AVEDA
THE ART AND SCIENCE OF PURE FLOWER AND PLANT ESSENCES

thicker, fuller hair is yours

97% naturally derived invati™ solutions for thinning hair
REDUCES HAIR LOSS BY 33%

2014/15
CoolBrands.uk.com

Aveda

A pioneer in environmental and social responsibility, Aveda has been crafting high-performance, professional botanical haircare and skincare products for over 30 years.

Connecting beauty, wellbeing and the environment, Aveda has the art and science of pure flower and plant essences at its core. All its products are alive with the life force of plants, professionally developed, clinically tested and go to exceptional lengths to respect the earth. Its environmental leadership and responsibility make Aveda a pioneer in the green cosmetics world. It unites nearly 7,000 salons and spas worldwide in sharing the Aveda mission: 'Beauty is as beauty does'.

AVEDA
THE ART AND SCIENCE OF PURE FLOWER AND PLANT ESSENCES

aveda.co.uk

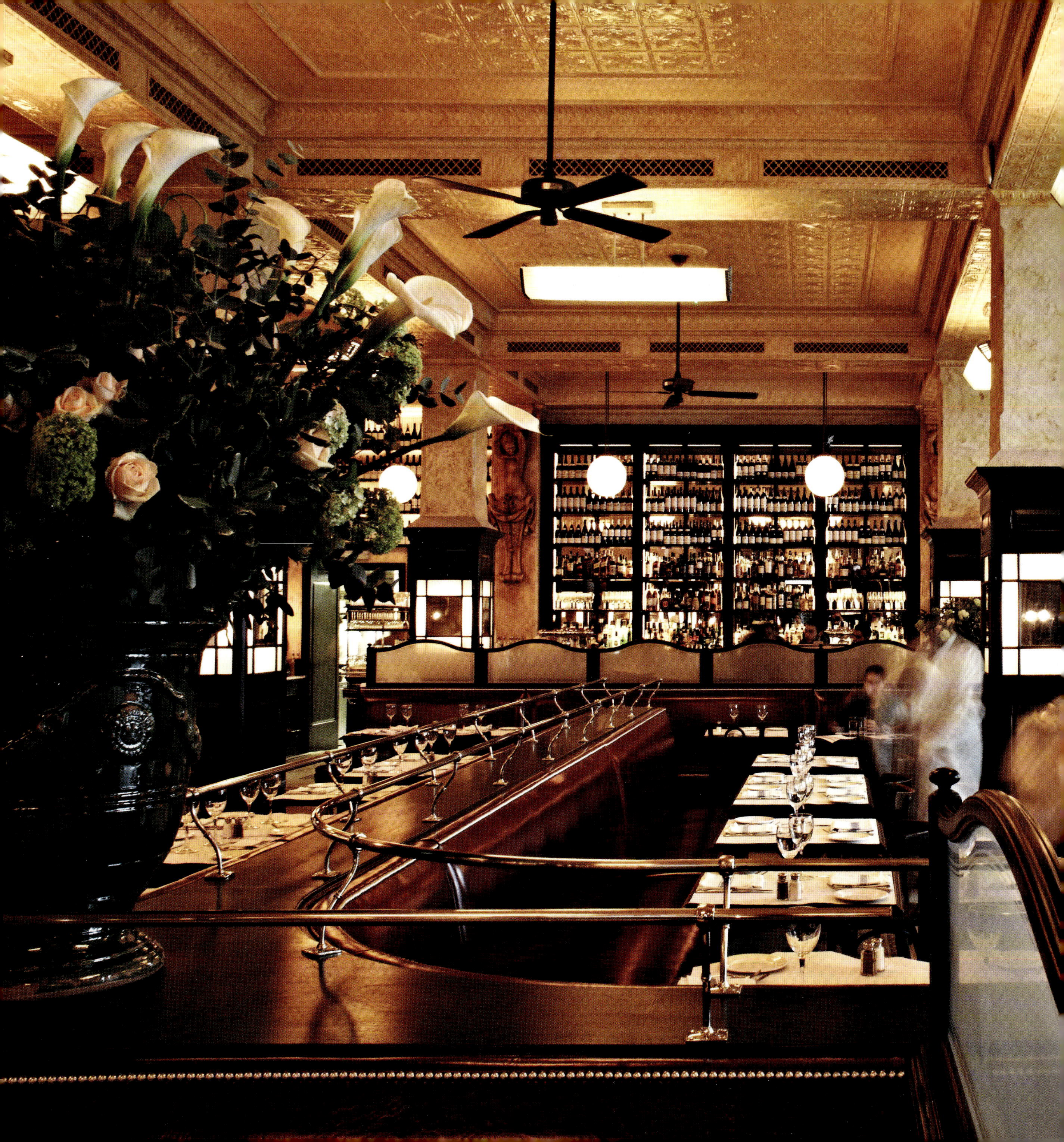

Balthazar

Following the huge success of the original restaurant in New York, Keith McNally opened Balthazar in the heart of London's Covent Garden in 2013.

With the egalitarian appeal of the brasserie, Balthazar London has something for everyone, all day long: breakfast, lunch, afternoon tea, dinner and weekend brunch. Keith McNally has endeavoured to remain true to the New York original, where bistro food, good wine, stylish cocktails and friendly service are the order of the day. The menu boasts an abundance of fruits de mer and classical French brasserie and bistro dishes. As in New York, a Balthazar boulangerie is housed next door.

balthazarlondon.com

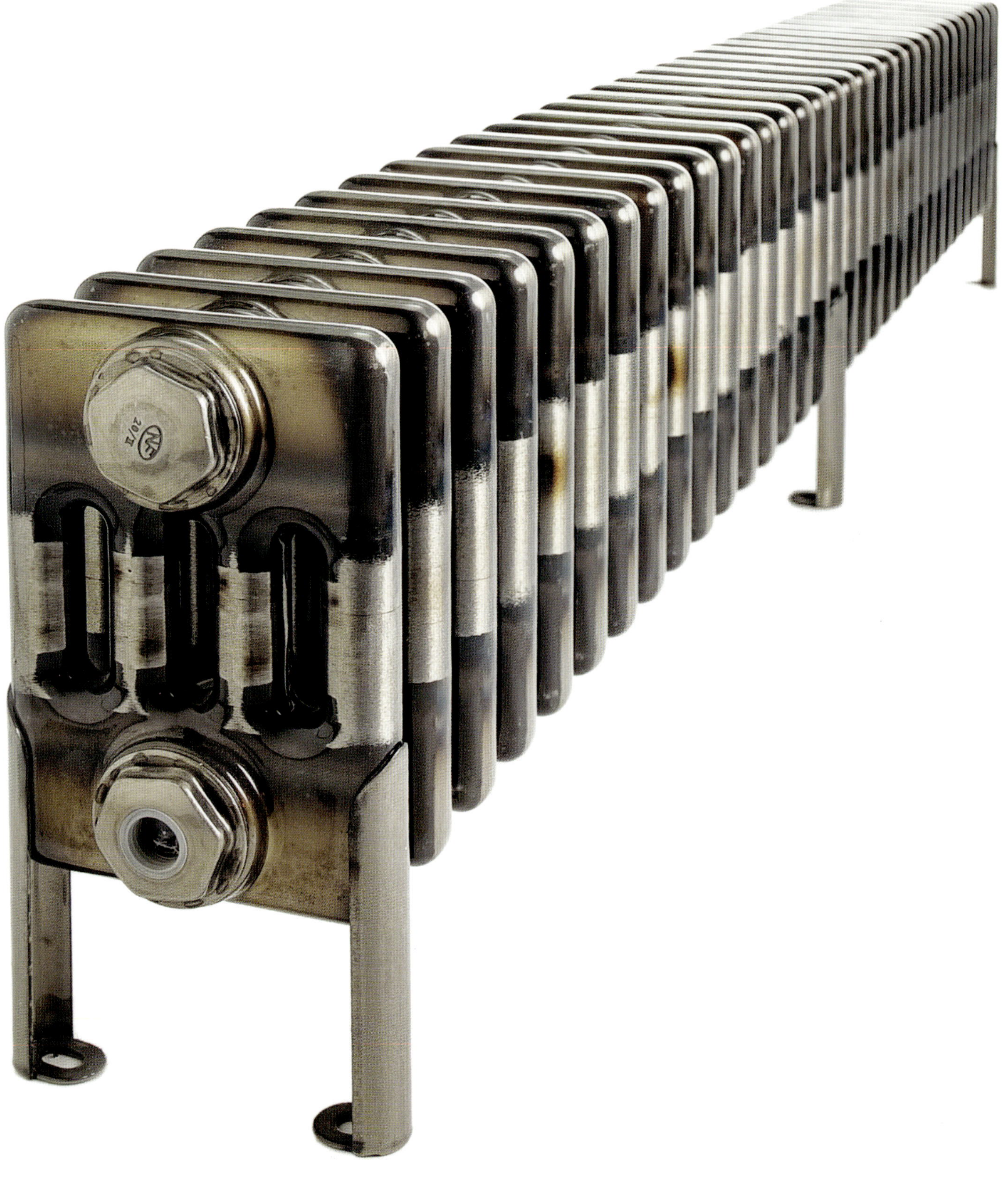

2014/15
CoolBrands.uk.com

Bisque

Leading interiors brand Bisque has a unique passion – to offer beautiful but practical radiators in the most exciting styles, colours and shapes.

Founded 35 years ago Bisque's passion for beautiful, high quality radiators remains undimmed. Whether it is statement pieces, eco-friendly ranges or elegant bathroom designs, it always strives for the 'four Ps': Pedigree, Proportion, Purity and Performance. Driven by enthusiastic people who understand how radiators can complement gorgeous interiors, Bisque's radiators can be found in locations ranging from The Shard to Highgrove House. It continues to work with the best manufacturers and designers to source the very latest designs.

bisque.co.uk

BISQUE

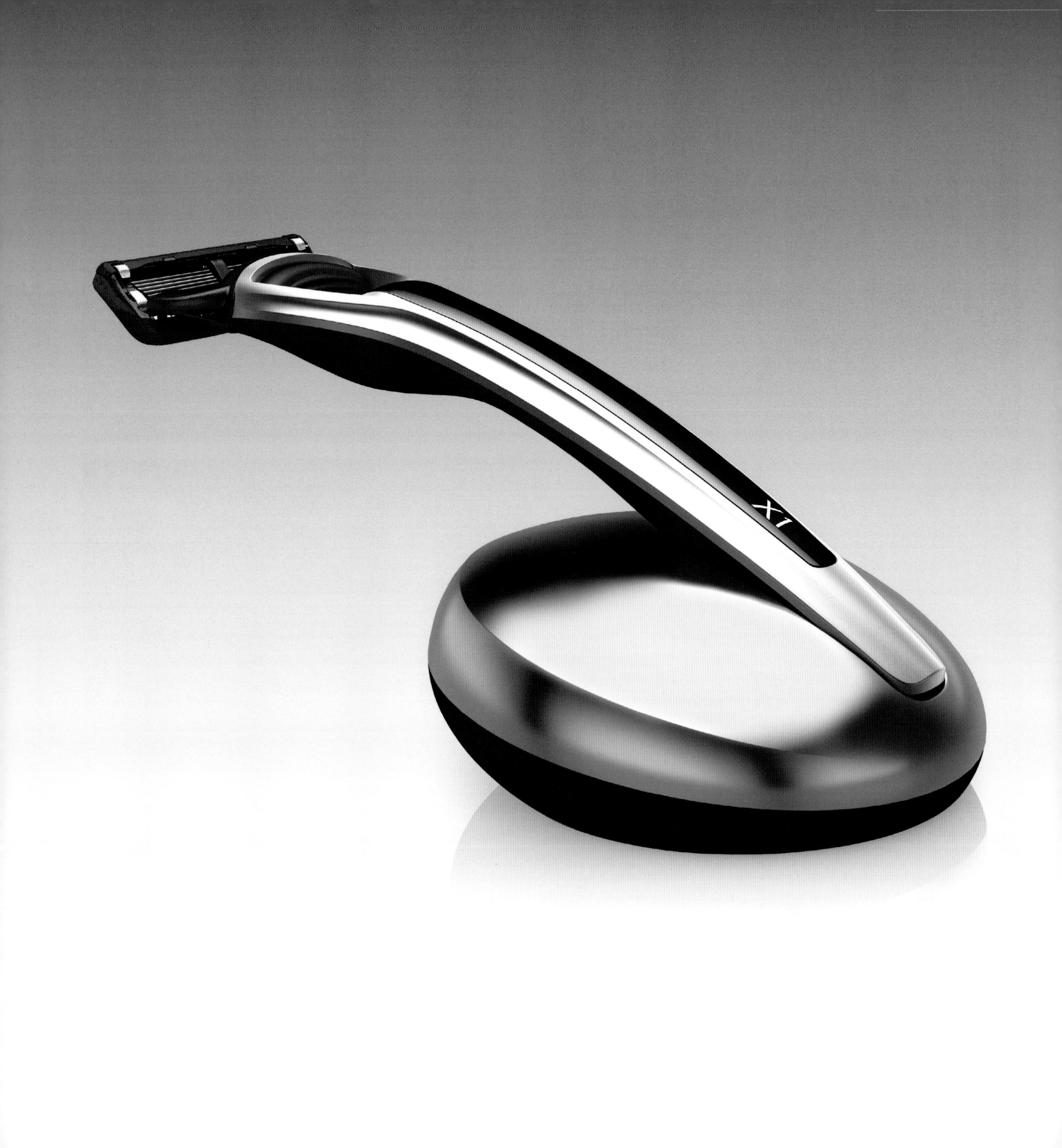
X1

2014/15
CoolBrands.uk.com

Bolin Webb

Where design and innovation meet performance, Bolin Webb provides contemporary grooming for men, and proves the razor in your bathroom can look and feel great.

Bolin Webb brings inspired design to the world of shaving with its UK-made R1 and X1 razors, which boast a quality automotive finish and a tactile grip, fitted with blades from Gillette. The award-winning company extends its fresh product range with an innovative set of razor stands and travel accessories, combining design and function with the careful use of selected materials. This young company sells its eye-catching products in premium retailers worldwide.

BOLIN•WEBB

bolinwebb.com

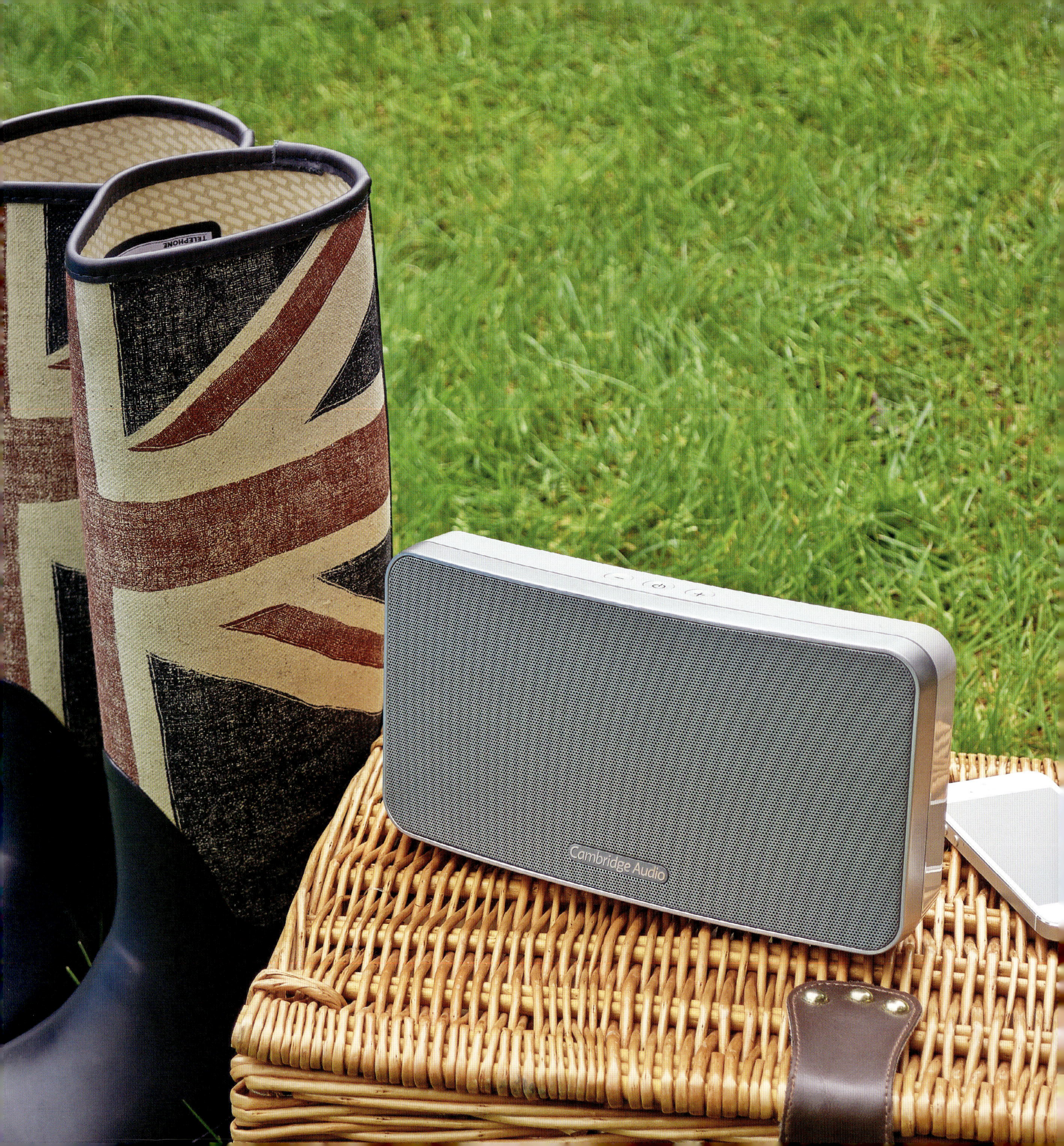
Cambridge Audio

2014/15
CoolBrands.uk.com

Cambridge Audio

Creating technically excellent audio equipment since the 1960s, Cambridge Audio's design teams have one motivation: to create dynamic, powerful products that indulge their customers with perfect sound.

The Cambridge Audio team is comprised of music lovers. This key musical passion enables them to deliver hi-fi systems and wireless speakers that sound stunning, whether in the home, at work, or on the move. London's iconic Southbank is where every single component and circuit is custom developed to meet stringent requirements of quality, detail and design. It is following this process that allows Cambridge Audio to create products that exude fantastic sound.

Cambridge Audio

cambridgeaudio.com

ONE MILLION
CHAPEL DOWN
BLANC DE BLANCS
2007
RADITIONAL BOTTLE FERMENTED
TENTERDEN ENGLAND
CHAPEL DOWN
BLANC DE BLANCS
TENTERDEN ENGLAND

2014/15
CoolBrands.uk.com

Chapel Down

Chapel Down embodies what is cool about England, with its fresh, innovative approach to premium sparkling wine.

Produced in Kent using grapes from across the South East, Chapel Down is England's leading wine producer and winner of an impressive array of awards. With a mission to surprise and delight, Chapel Down quickly gained support from leading chefs such as Gordon Ramsay and Jamie Oliver, as well as hitting the headlines for producing the country's largest bottle of sparkling wine. Chapel Down is pushing the boundaries in English wine and is definitely a reason to be patriotic.

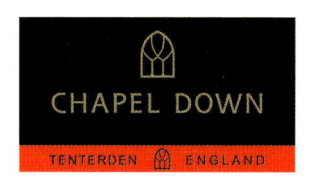

chapeldown.com

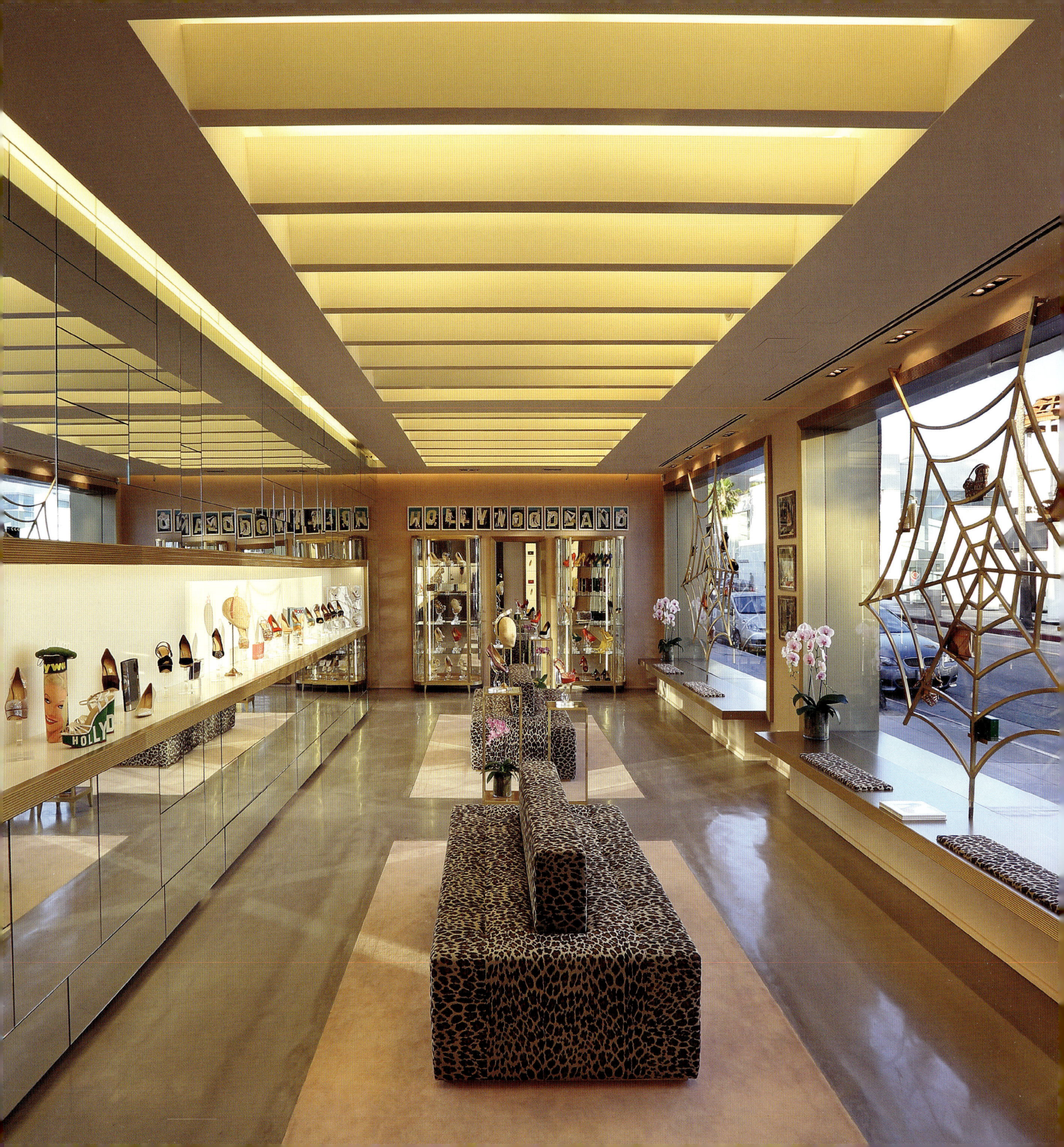
HOLLY

2014/15
CoolBrands.uk.com

Charlotte Olympia

Sparked by a love of fashion and the art of corsetry, Charlotte Olympia's London-based shoe brand is synonymous with classic sophistication and meticulous attention to detail.

Inspired by a bygone era of old Hollywood glamour, Charlotte Olympia's iconic styles, such as the Dolly with its signature 'island' platform, are in keeping with the brand's feminine design philosophy. All designs are handcrafted in Italy using only the finest materials and each shoe is finished with a signature gold spider's web on the sole. With a growing international retail presence, Charlotte Olympia has stores in Mayfair, Manhattan, Beverly Hills, Miami, Hong Kong and Dubai.

charlotteolympia.com

CHARLOTTE OLYMPIA

What better time than now?

200 years crafting a cognac with the perfect blend of aromas, so you can enjoy this moment.

COURVOISIER
HERE'S TO NOW

drinkaware.co.uk for the facts

2014/15
CoolBrands.uk.com

Photography by Jillian Lochner (represented by Germaine Walker)

Courvoisier

Courvoisier has been handcrafting award-winning cognac for over 200 years and remains the only cognac house to be awarded 'Le Prestige de la France'.

Courvoisier believes that life should be enjoyed now. That's why it has spent 200 years crafting cognac with the perfect blend of aromas so that every second can be lived to the full. The new 'Here's to Now' campaign seeks to challenge the 'rules' surrounding the cognac category, highlighting the more unexpected and sociable occasions where Courvoisier can be enjoyed. The spontaneity behind the campaign is then accentuated with straplines including 'What better time than now?'

courvoisier.com

CRUSSH
FIT FOOD

2014/15
CoolBrands.uk.com

Crussh

Founded in 1998 on Cornhill in London, Crussh is the leading juice, smoothie and healthy fast food retailer.

Making food 'healthier, tastier and easier' is at the very heart of everything that Crussh does. A constant innovator and leader of healthy food trends, Crussh is often imitated. Known for its signature healthpots, zero noodles and green juices, Crussh is the destination of choice for anyone with an interest in healthy eating. All juices are freshly pressed, smoothies are made-to-order in every store, and the range of 'fit food' is handmade every day in Crussh's own kitchen.

crussh.com

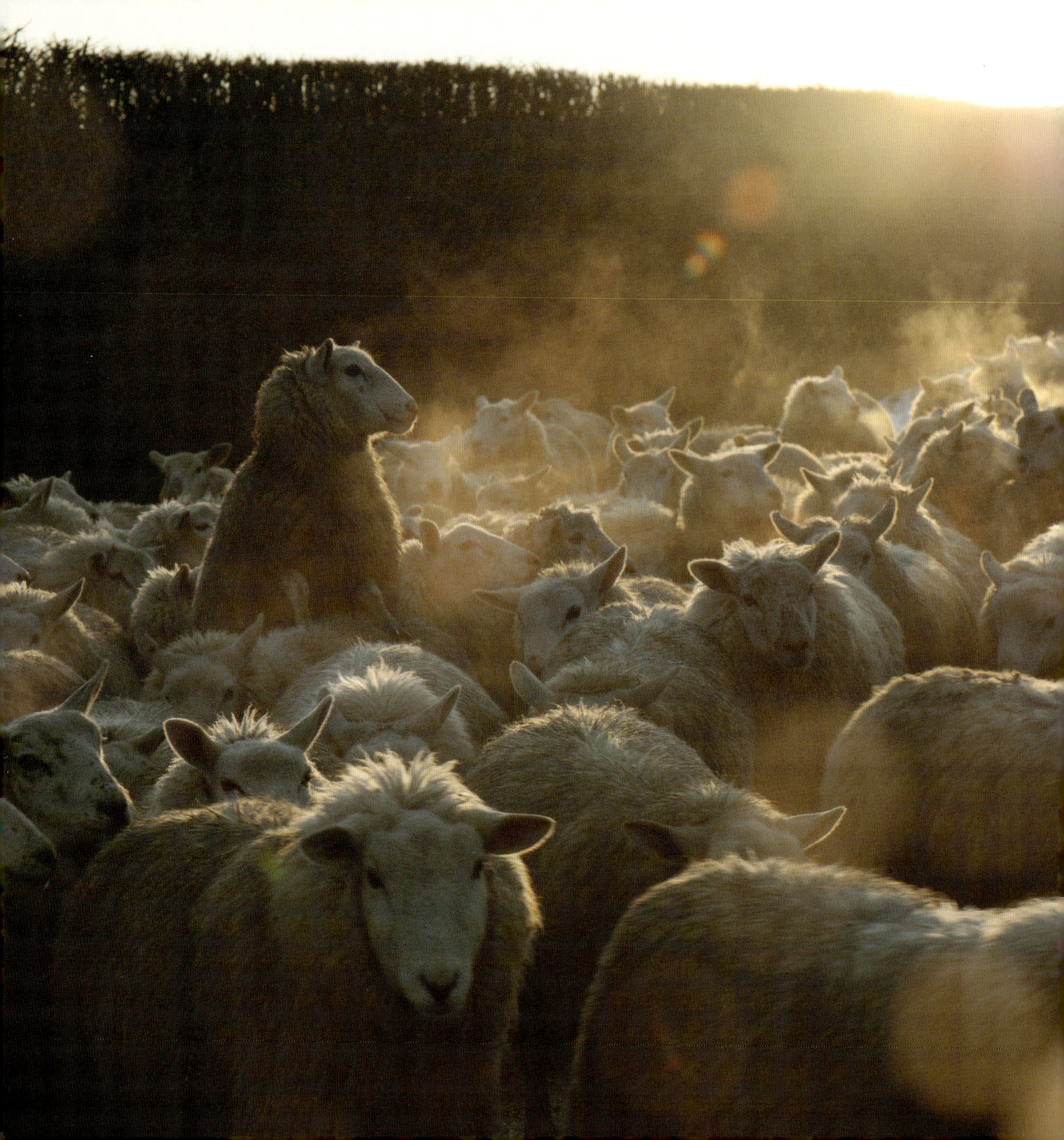

2014/15
CoolBrands.uk.com

Daylesford

With the simple aim of making the best food possible, Daylesford is an organic family farm dedicated to changing the way we eat.

Having farmed organically for more than 30 years, Daylesford brings the best of the season straight from its farm to your fork, combining the freshest ingredients with artisan skills and a little flair to create award-winning organic food that is as good as it tastes. Daylesford works with the seasons to rear contented animals, grow fruit and vegetables, and make award-winning cheeses, breads and cakes – all ready to be enjoyed in Daylesford's kitchens, or yours.

daylesford

daylesford.com

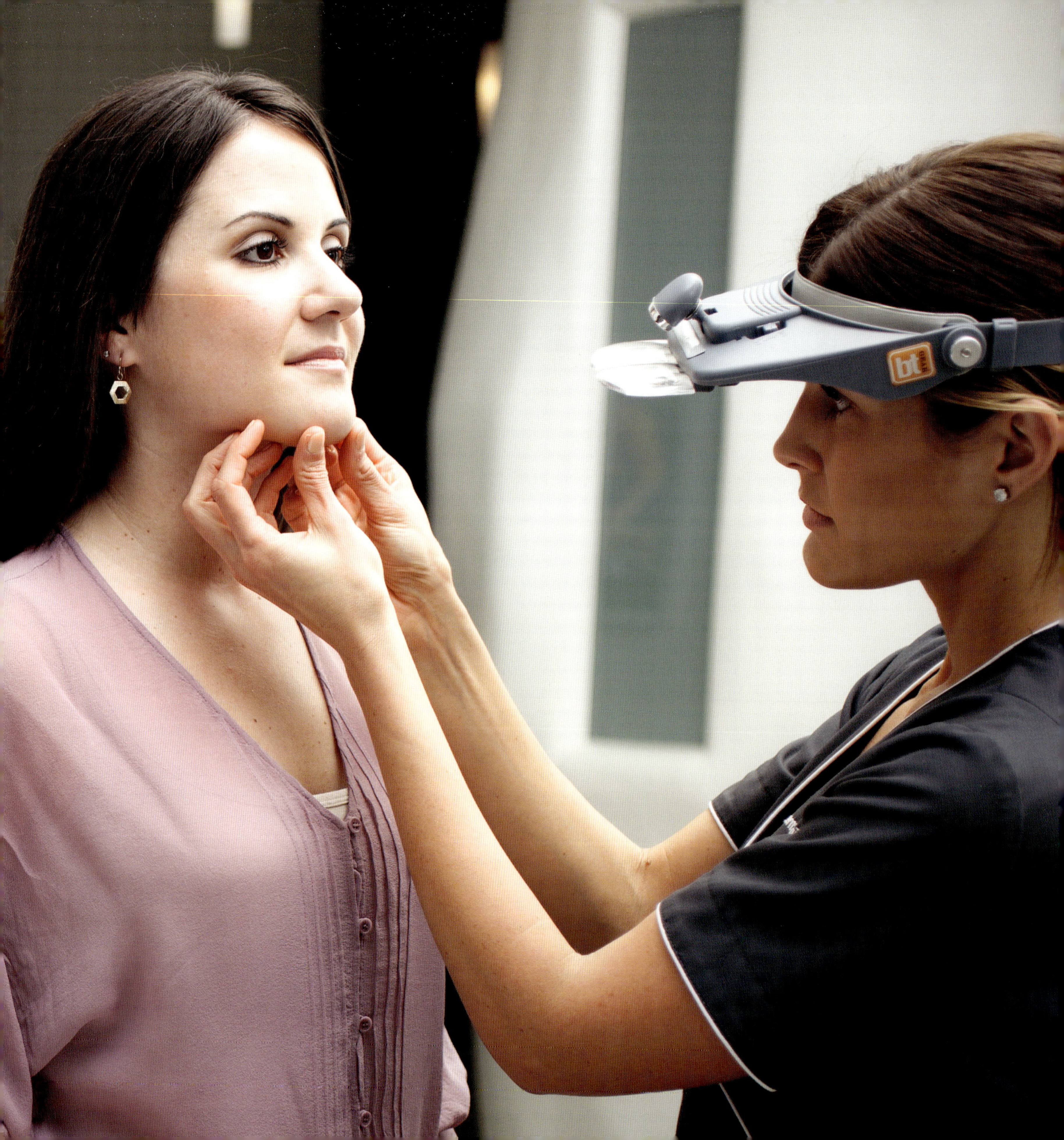
bt

face mapping®

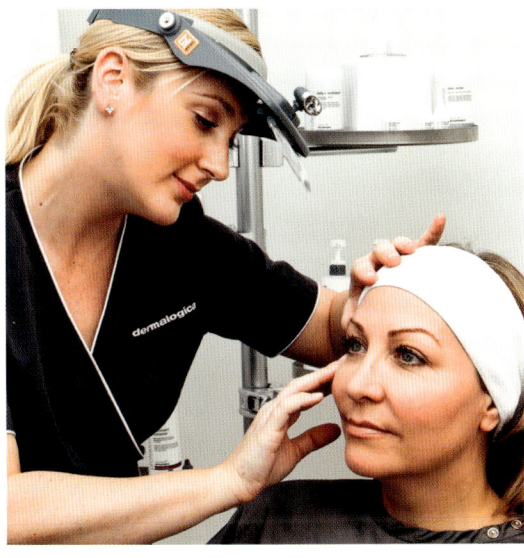

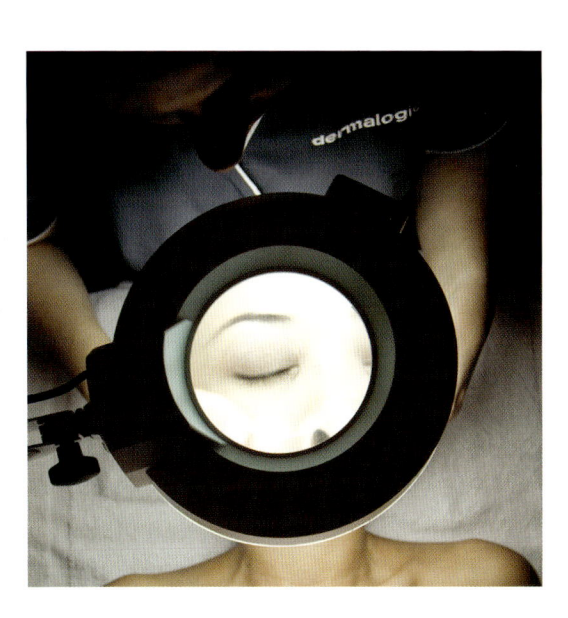

Dermalogica

Dermalogica puts skin therapists first – leading the creation of the most effective, and unique, treatment concepts in the industry.

All skin has a story and, at Dermalogica, it's told with Face Mapping®. Inspired by its educational roots, Dermalogica skin therapists use the unique and interactive Face Mapping® skin analysis technique to deliver skin health results for clients that keep them coming back for more. With 30 years of developing products that challenge industry standards under its belt, Dermalogica owes its success to the unwavering support of the skin care professional and the service they provide their clients.

dermalogica.com

Constance Halaveli, Maldives

2014/15
CoolBrands.uk.com

Madinat Jumeirah, Dubai

Destinology

Taking luxury travel to new levels, Destinology curators search the globe for exclusive hotels for a discerning clientele, ensuring its portfolio features every leading hotel and resort.

With expert consultants regularly visiting the resorts on offer and cutting-edge web, mobile and tablet sites featuring Google virtual tours to guide clients through a vast range of luxury hotels, Destinology guarantees the very best. A winner at the British Travel Awards in 2012 and 2013, Destinology has been nominated an unprecedented 14 times this year. The flagship retail store in Wilmslow, Cheshire is unlike any travel agency seen before, with five star finishes and award-winning customer service.

destinology.co.uk

DESTINOLOGY
EXPERTS IN LUXURY TRAVEL

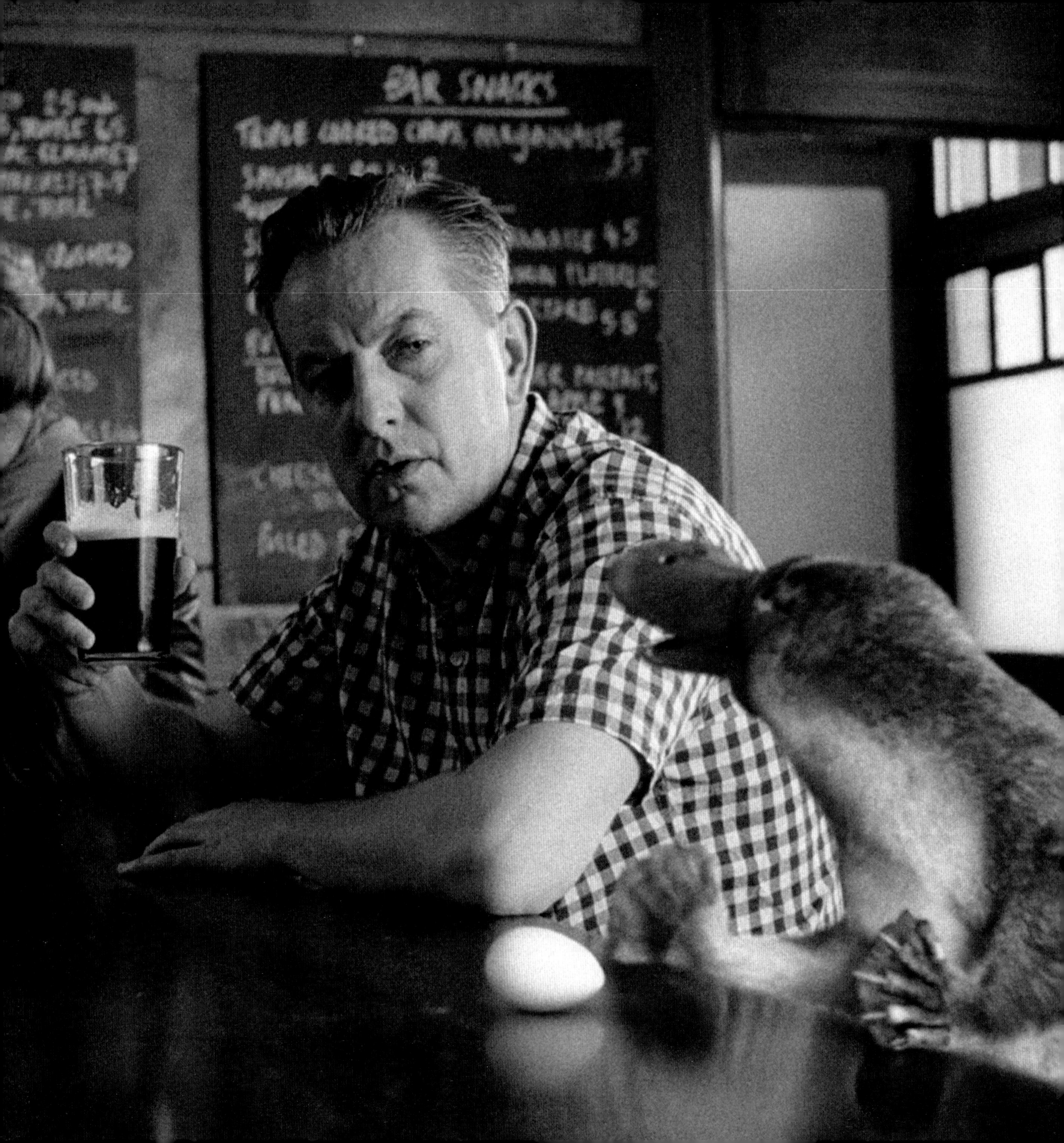
BAR SNACKS
TRIPLE COOKED CHIPS, MAYONNAISE
3.5

2014/15
CoolBrands.uk.com

Knockout rates for Personal Loans

4.0% APR representative

Now available for loans between £7,000 and £25,000

Apply in minutes

Available to 1st Account customers only

Kapow!

We are to banks what the platypus is to mammals.
The unexpected bank

firstdirect.com
0800 24 24 24, always open.

If a tomato is a fruit, then we're a bank.
The unexpected bank

firstdirect.com
0800 24 24 24, always open.

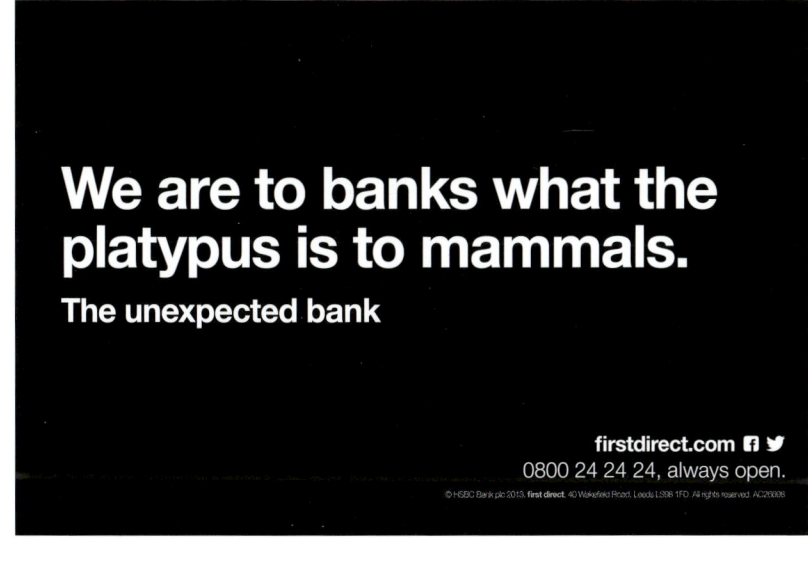

first direct

With the most satisfied customers, who recommend their bank more than the customers of any other, first direct is as fresh today as when it launched 25 years ago.

More than one million customers continue to enjoy the best banking service around and first direct's recent advertising campaign featuring Barry the Platypus has attracted a new generation of customers. With a joined up telephone and online service, first direct doesn't see itself as a telephone bank or an internet bank, but simply as a better bank for its customers, whatever the channel. As of October 2014, it will have been open continuously for more than 9,000 days.

firstdirect.com

first direct

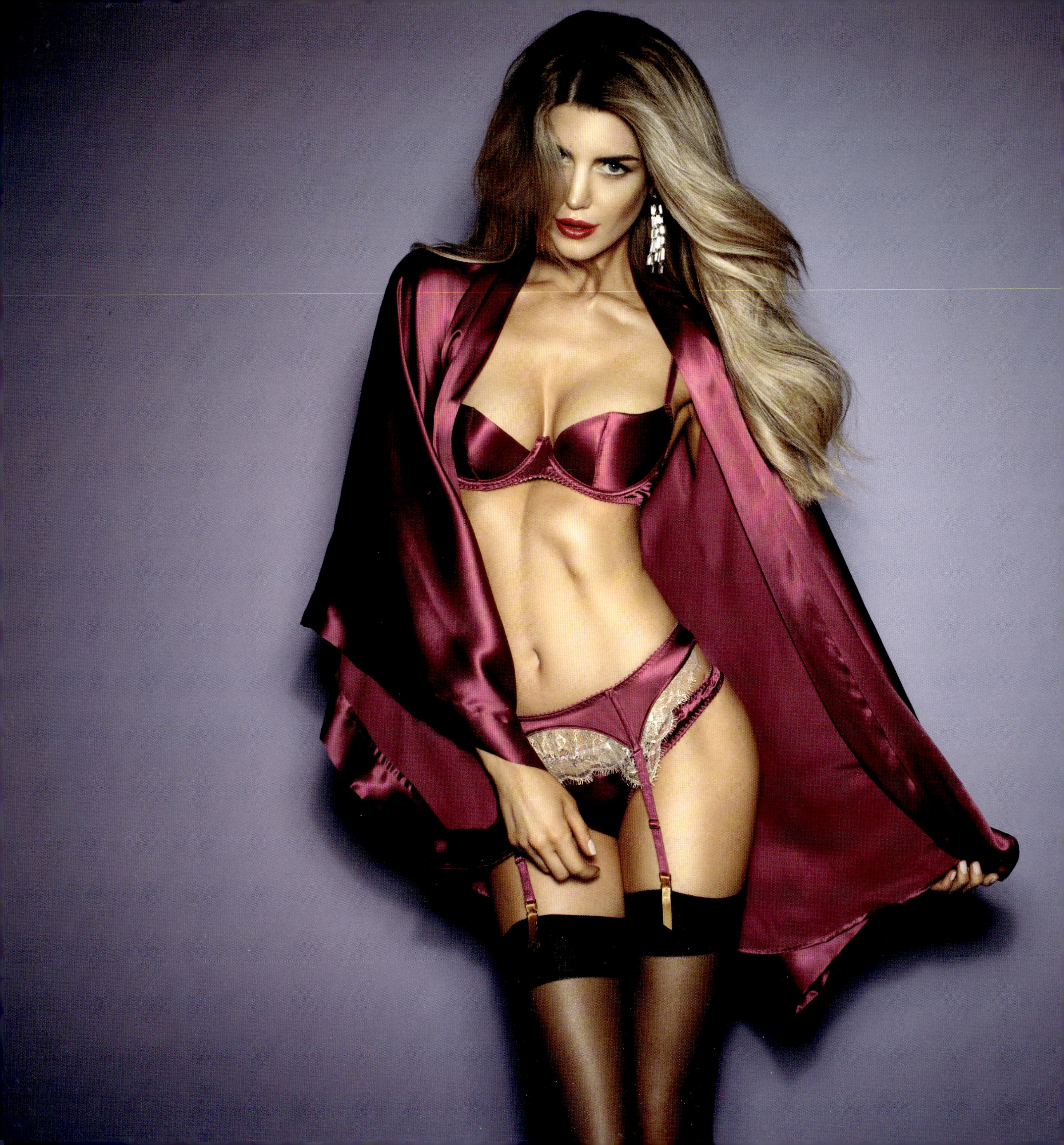

2014/15
CoolBrands.uk.com

Fred & Ginger

Launched during London Fashion Week in 2007, Fred & Ginger is quickly becoming one of the most desirable lingerie brands in the world.

Founded by Creative Director, Victoria Holt, Fred & Ginger evolved from a desire to create beautiful products for a market that appreciates design detail, quality, luxury and originality. Each Fred & Ginger garment is lovingly made in the UK, using the finest fabrics and trims. In a time where fashion is throwaway, the brand pays homage to an era when quality and finesse were paramount with ranges inspired by old Hollywood glamour.

Fred & Ginger London

fredandginger.com

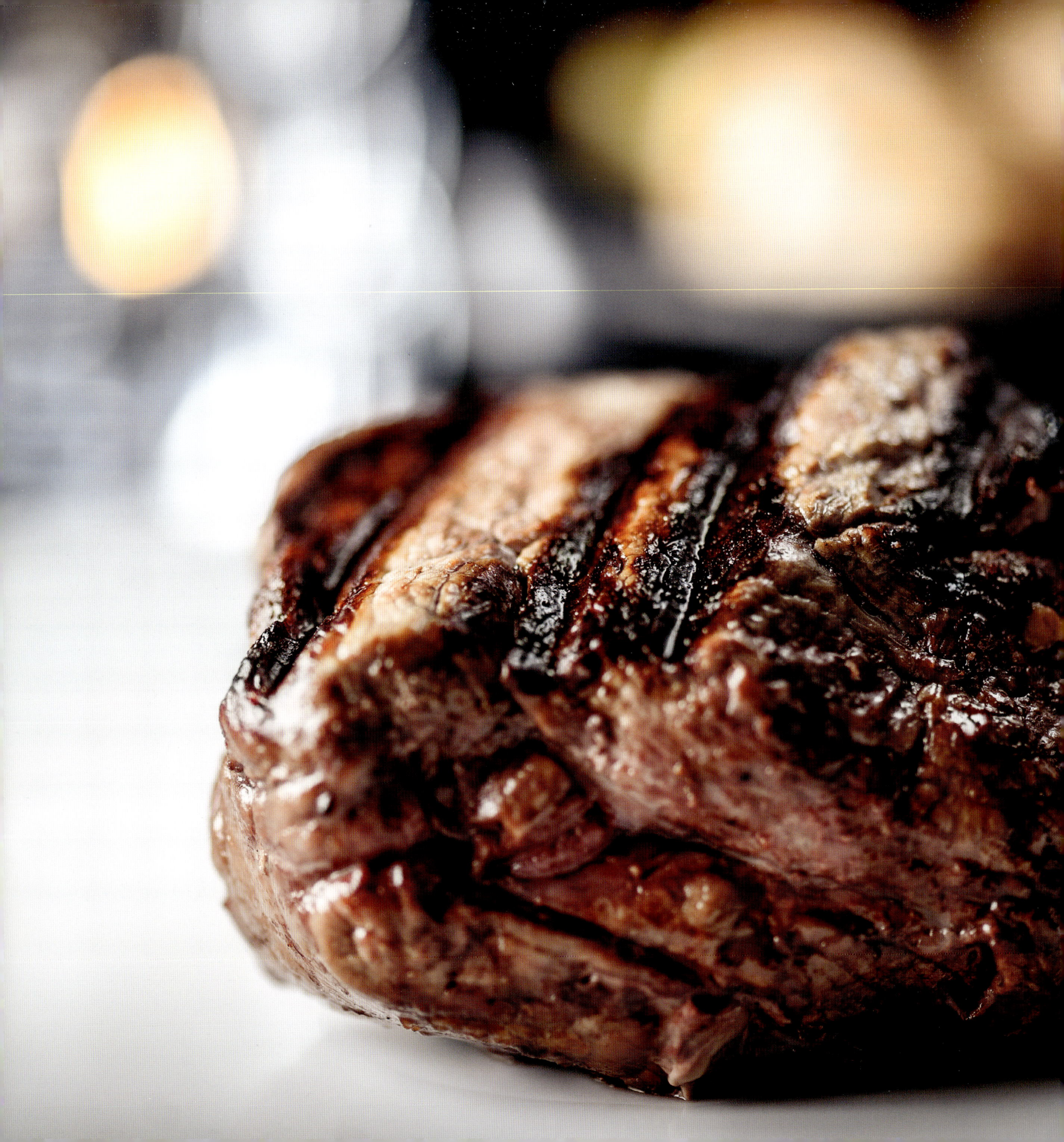

2014/15
CoolBrands.uk.com

Gaucho

Gaucho believes that every guest should experience the true essence of Argentine life – its food, its wine, its culture and, most importantly, the passion of the people.

Renowned for serving the best steaks in London, Gaucho boasts cuisine that is the benchmark for modern 'Nuevo Latino' dining. Gaucho plays on its traditional Argentine roots by forging close links with Polo and by championing Argentine wine and beef. Its cattle are selected by a team of experts on the ground in Argentina, where modern farming technology, 150 years of farming history and the absence of pesticides combine to make for the extraordinary beef served in the restaurants.

GAUCHO

gauchorestaurants.co.uk

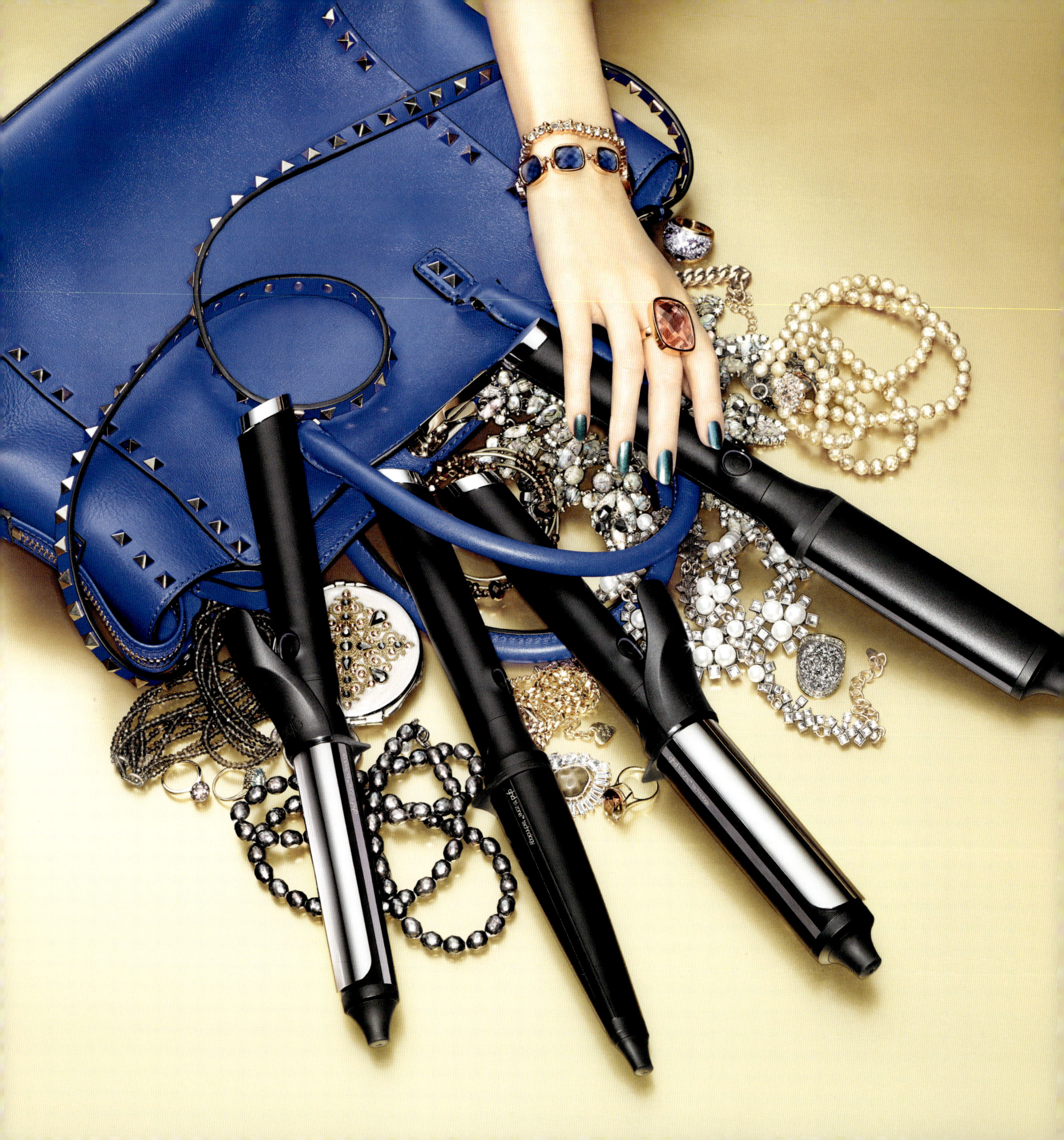

ghd

Committed to product innovation and improvements in technology, ghd offers a range of market leading professional hair styling tools that deliver a good hair day, every day.

At launch, ghd's ceramic styling irons initiated a huge following that has grown over the last 14 years. Now at the forefront of the fashion styling sector, it is renowned as one of the leading hair styling brands around the world. This year, ghd curve – a new range of curling tools used to create long-lasting curls and waves – will join the current line-up of five hair stylers, two hairdryers, a range of styling brushes and wet-line.

ghdhair.com

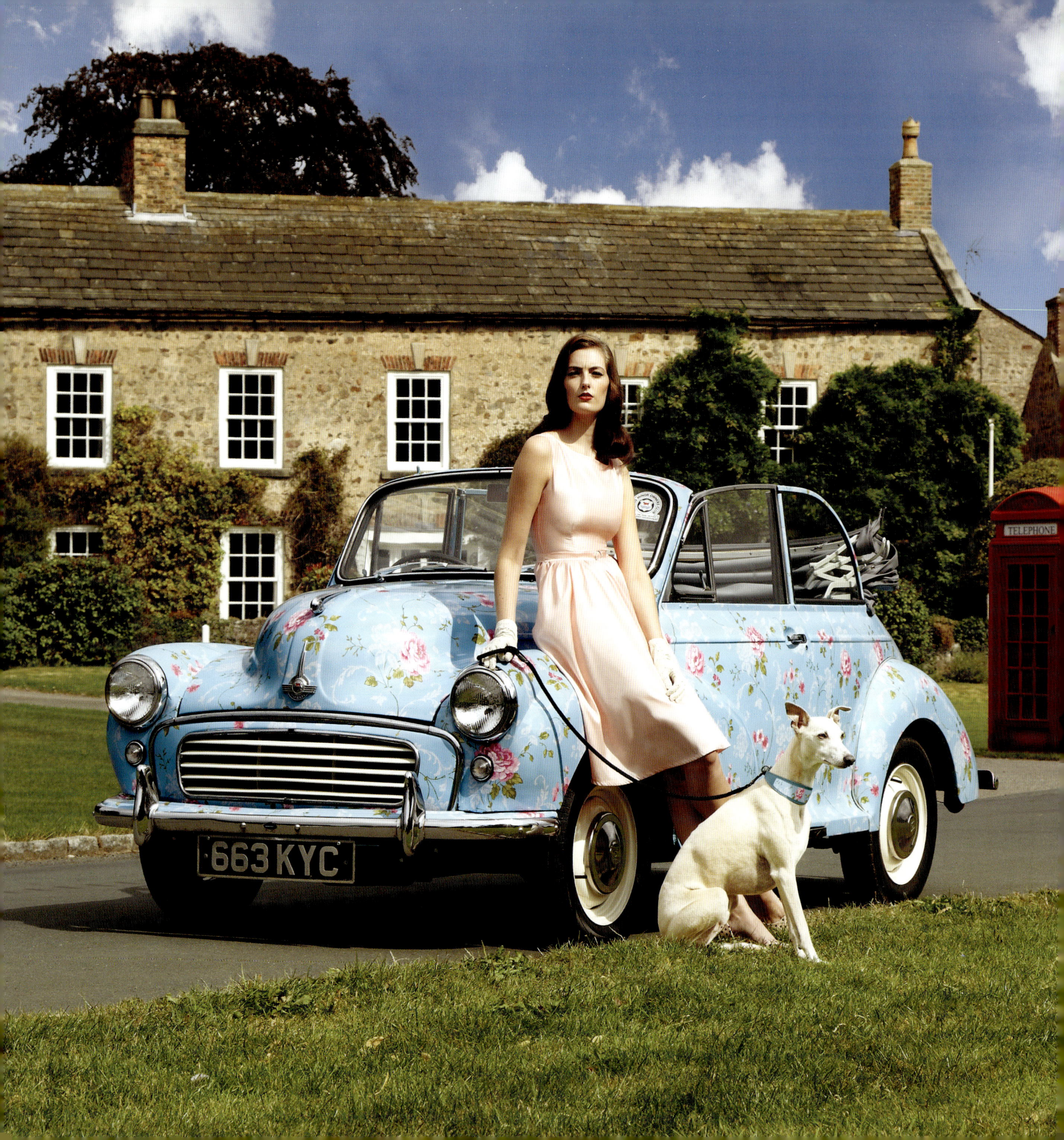
TELEPHONE
663 KYC

2014/15
CoolBrands.uk.com

Graham & Brown

Since 1946, Graham & Brown has been doing things differently. From its humble beginnings in post-war Blackburn, it has become the leading light in wallpaper worldwide.

The resurgence in wallpaper is impossible to ignore. It's topical, and its revival owes a lot to Graham & Brown. Its innovative approach and partnerships with design luminaries such as Marcel Wanders, Kelly Hoppen, Steve Leung and the Victoria and Albert Museum as well as the launch of the New Wave Collective are at the heart of the brand's Made of Design ethos.

GRAHAM & BROWN
EST. 1946

grahambrown.com

GREEN & BLACK'S
ORGANIC
Milk Chocolate
with delicate flakes of Anglesey Sea Salt
37% Cocoa
e100g
GREEN&BLACK'S ORGANIC MILK CHOCOLATE WITH ANGLESEY SEA SALT
GREEN&BLACK'S SMOOTH AND CREAMY MILK CHOCOLATE
GREEN&BLACK'S COCOA-RICH MILK CHOCOLATE
GREEN&BLACK'S DARK CHOCOLATE WITH HAZELNUTS & CURRANTS

2014/15
CoolBrands.uk.com

Green & Black's Organic

As a premium chocolate brand, Green & Black's has stayed true to its organic and fairtrade principles, having long set a precedent for what makes 'real' chocolate.

Chocolate bars, gift boxes, Easter eggs, ice cream and hot chocolate – Green & Black's has a delicious array of chocolate, all made from the very best Trinitario cocoa beans from the Dominican Republic, with their unique flavour and aroma. Green & Black's ingredients make it who it is and its commitment to quality expands across everything that it sources. Currently 19 flavours are available across dark, milk and white chocolate. Which is your favourite?

GREEN
&BLACK'S
ORGANIC

greenandblacks.co.uk

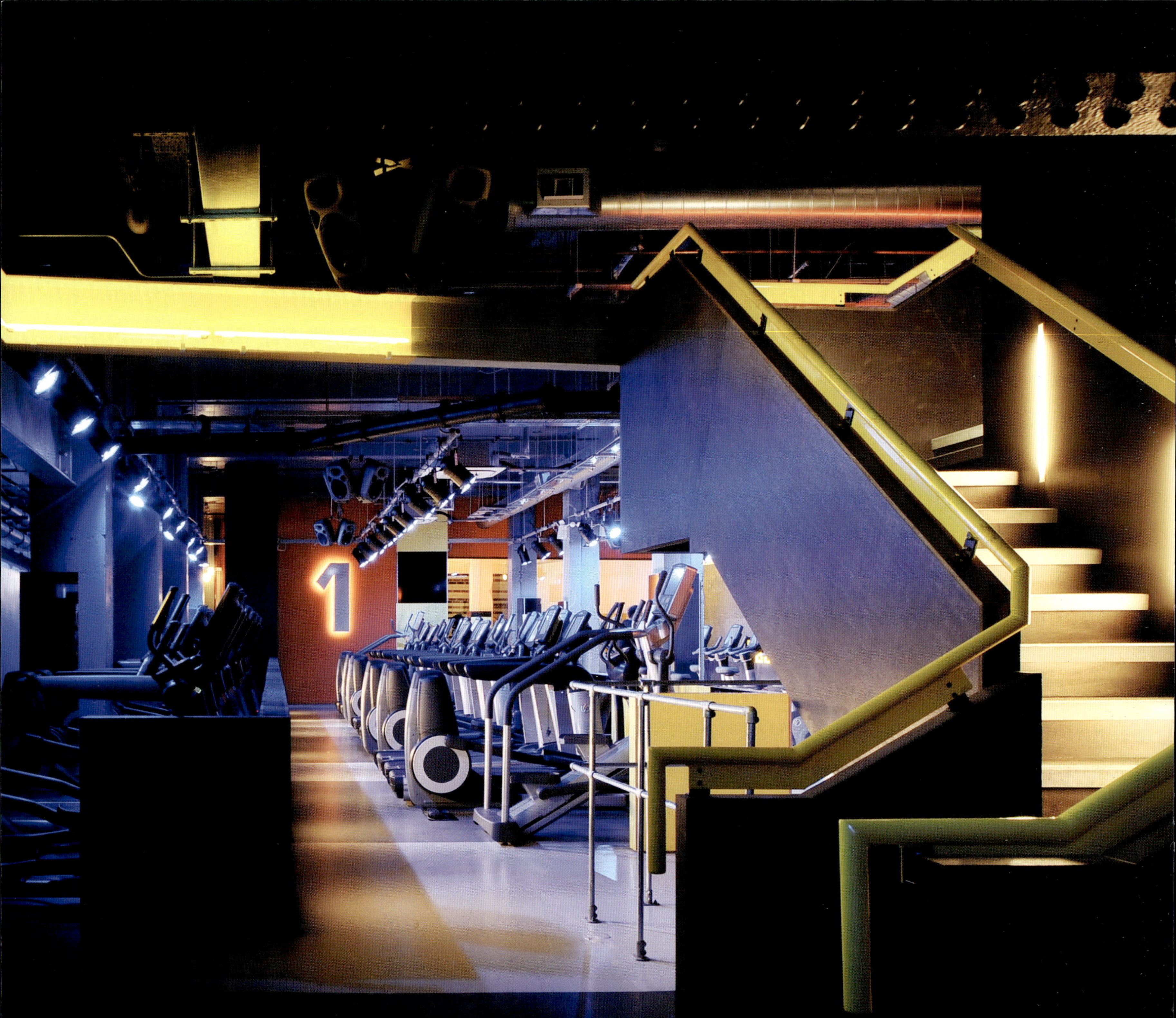
1

2014/15
CoolBrands.uk.com

GYMBOX

The unique combination of contemporary interiors, live DJs and extraordinary exercise classes makes GYMBOX the must-go place for fitness-savvy Londoners.

Since 2003, GYMBOX has redefined the way people experience fitness. Each gym interior is individually designed to ensure that the clubs look and feel unique. Mesmerising designs, extraordinary classes, nightly resident DJs and larger-than-life personal trainers are just a few of the reasons members come back to GYMBOX on a regular basis. Rave dancing, Karaoke Spinning and Twerk It Out are just a few of the hundreds of classes on offer.

gymbox.com

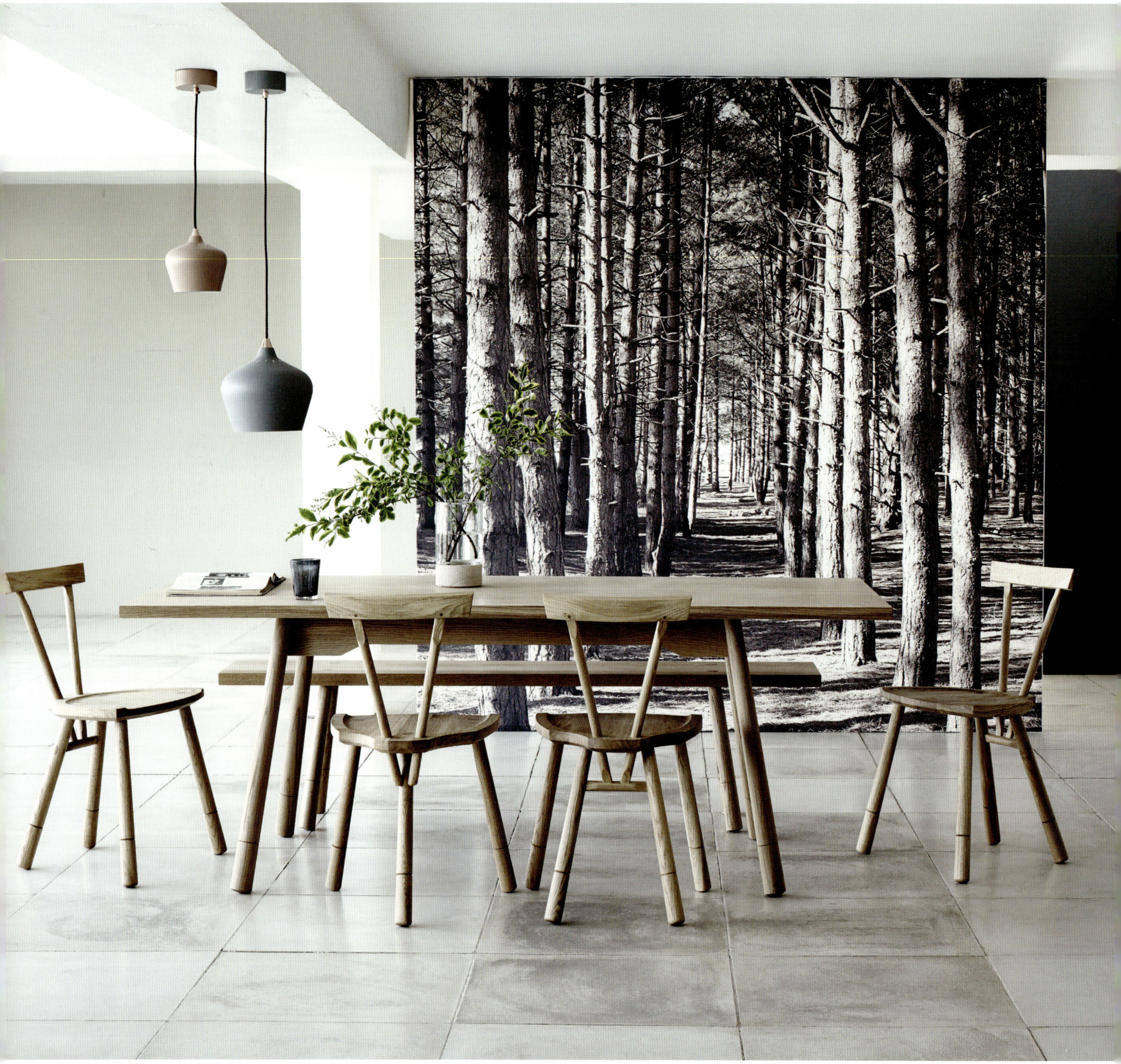

2014/15
CoolBrands.uk.com

Heal's

Good design. Well made. These two simple rules have guided Heal's directional collections for more than 200 years.

Starting out in 1810 as a maker of mattresses, Heal's has continuously applied a forward-thinking attitude towards design to secure a reputation as the home of modern and contemporary furniture in the UK. As well as promoting and mentoring design talent, it is known for placing a high value on innovation, craftsmanship and quality materials, so its customers can expect nothing less than the best.

HEAL'S

heals.co.uk

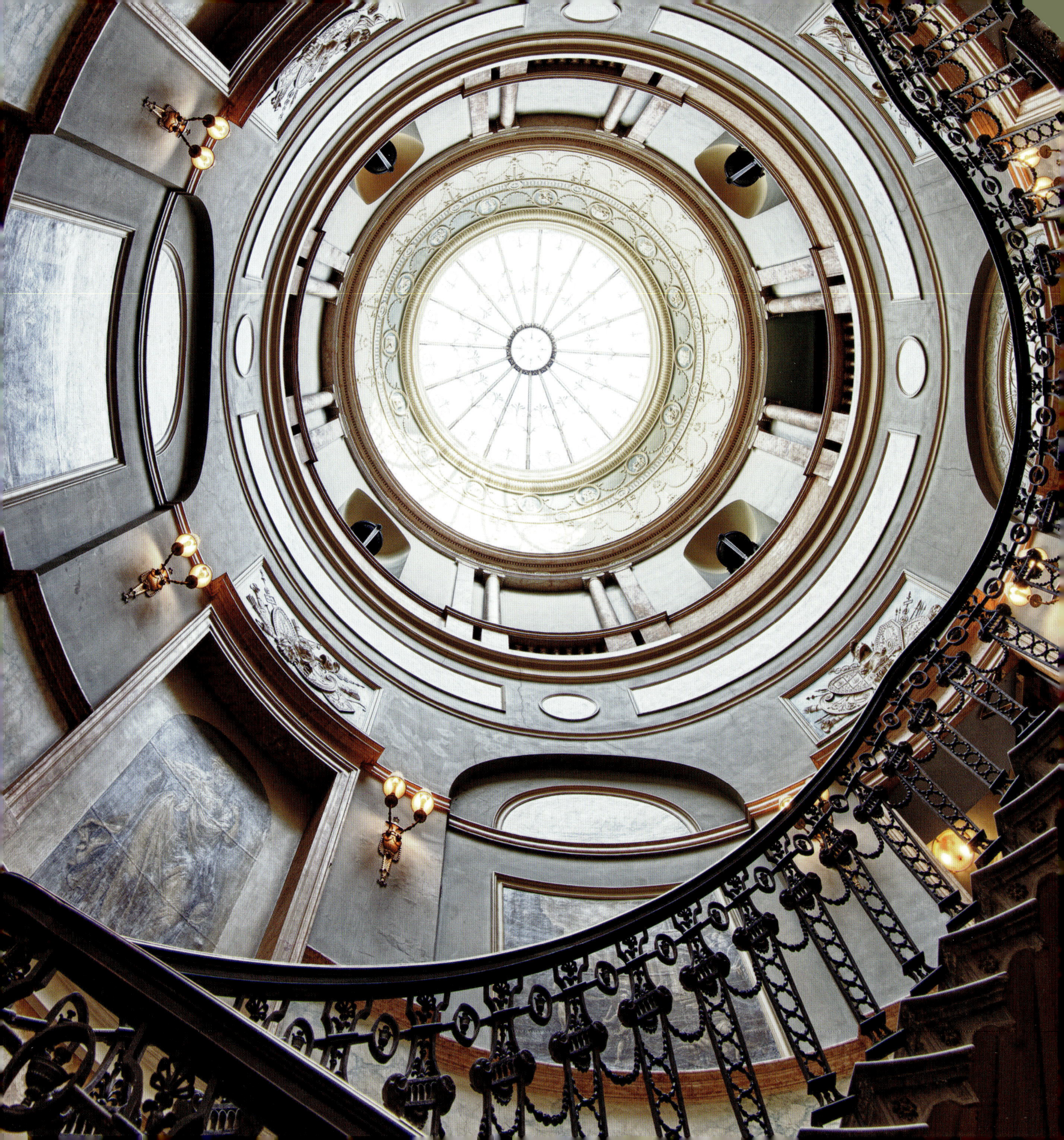

2014/15
CoolBrands.uk.com

Home House

One of central London's best-kept secrets, Home House Private Members' Club is a true home from home – an elegant oasis in the vibrant West End.

Located across three stunning Georgian townhouses in Portman Square, Home House is a melting pot of people from all cultures and professions who come together to meet friends, network and relax. House parties are legendary, intimate socials over afternoon tea are charming, while the energy and buzz of simmering chat and conversation over cocktails gives way to outbursts of revelry that are de rigeur for a late evening in the bars.

Home House

homehouse.co.uk

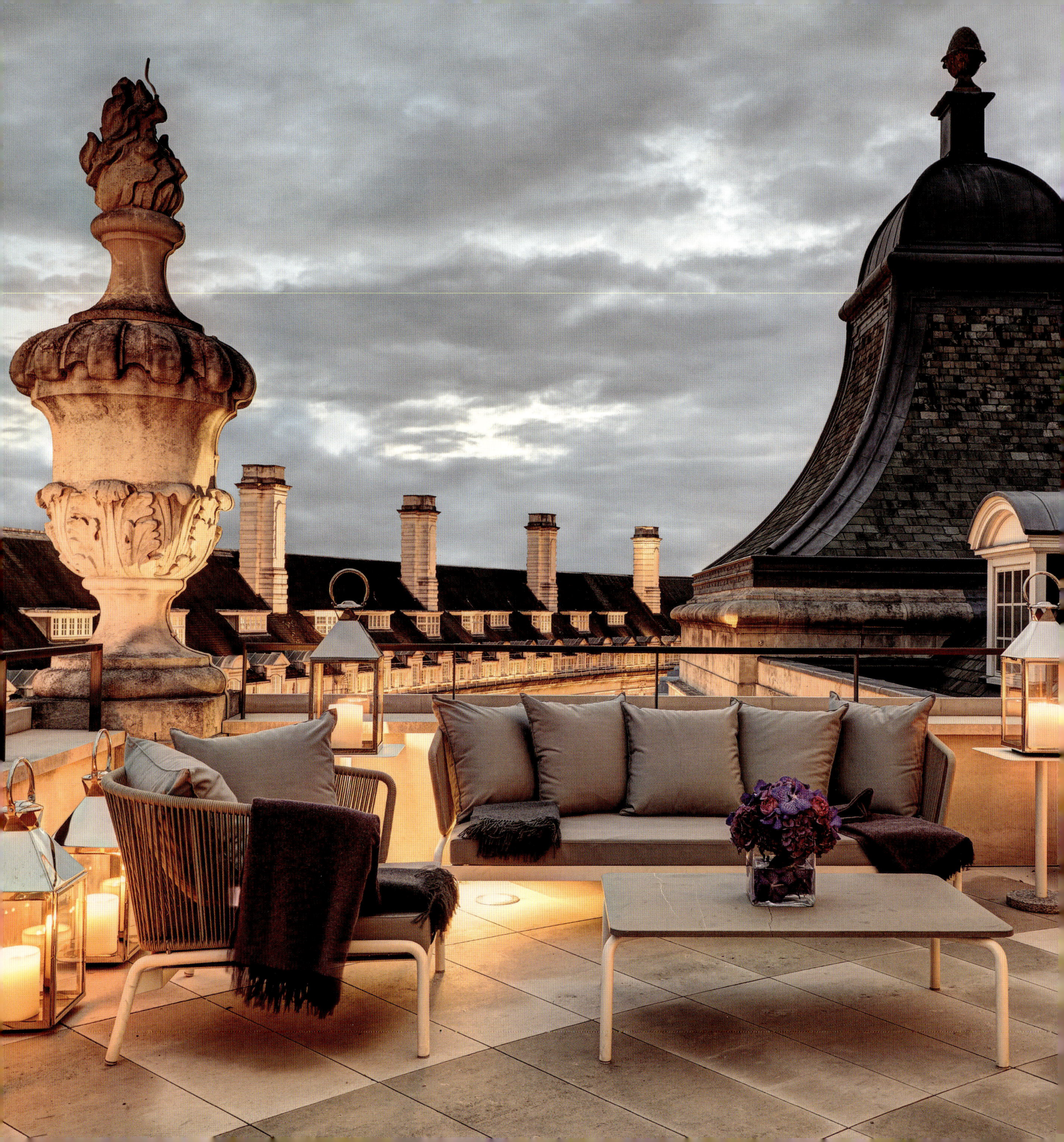

2014/15
CoolBrands.uk.com

Hotel Café Royal

In the heart of London's West End, Hotel Café Royal is where glamour and heritage meet elegant style and comfort.

Combining architectural heritage with contemporary design, Hotel Café Royal has been reincarnated as a luxury hotel with the elegance of Mayfair to the west and the creativity of Soho to the east. Grand historic areas have been sensitively restored while 160 guest rooms and suites (including six signature suites) have been created in a contemporary yet refined style. Continuing its celebrated legacy, the hotel offers a selection of restaurants and bars as well as the Akasha Holistic Wellbeing Centre.

HOTEL CAFÉ ROYAL
REGENT STREET, LONDON

hotelcaferoyal.com

Hotel du Vin
&
Bistro
CAMBRIDGE
Hotel du Vin
&
Bistro
CAMBRIDGE
Hotel du Vin
Do not accept any responsibility for loss or damage to any bicycles left against these railings
Hotel du Vi
&
Bistro

2014/15
CoolBrands.uk.com

Hotel du Vin

Simple yet sophisticated. Informal yet luxurious. Elegant yet unpretentious – and always quintessentially British. This is the very essence of Hotel du Vin.

Each Hotel du Vin has a unique character shaped by the architecture, history and sensitive conversion of the building. And at the heart of each, bistros serve French classics with a British twist, while cosy, low-lit bars offer many of the world's finest and best-kept secret wines, thanks to close relationships with vineyards and winemakers. At each and every Hotel du Vin, guests will appreciate a wholehearted commitment to doing the simple things, brilliantly.

Hotel du Vin & Bistro

hotelduvin.com

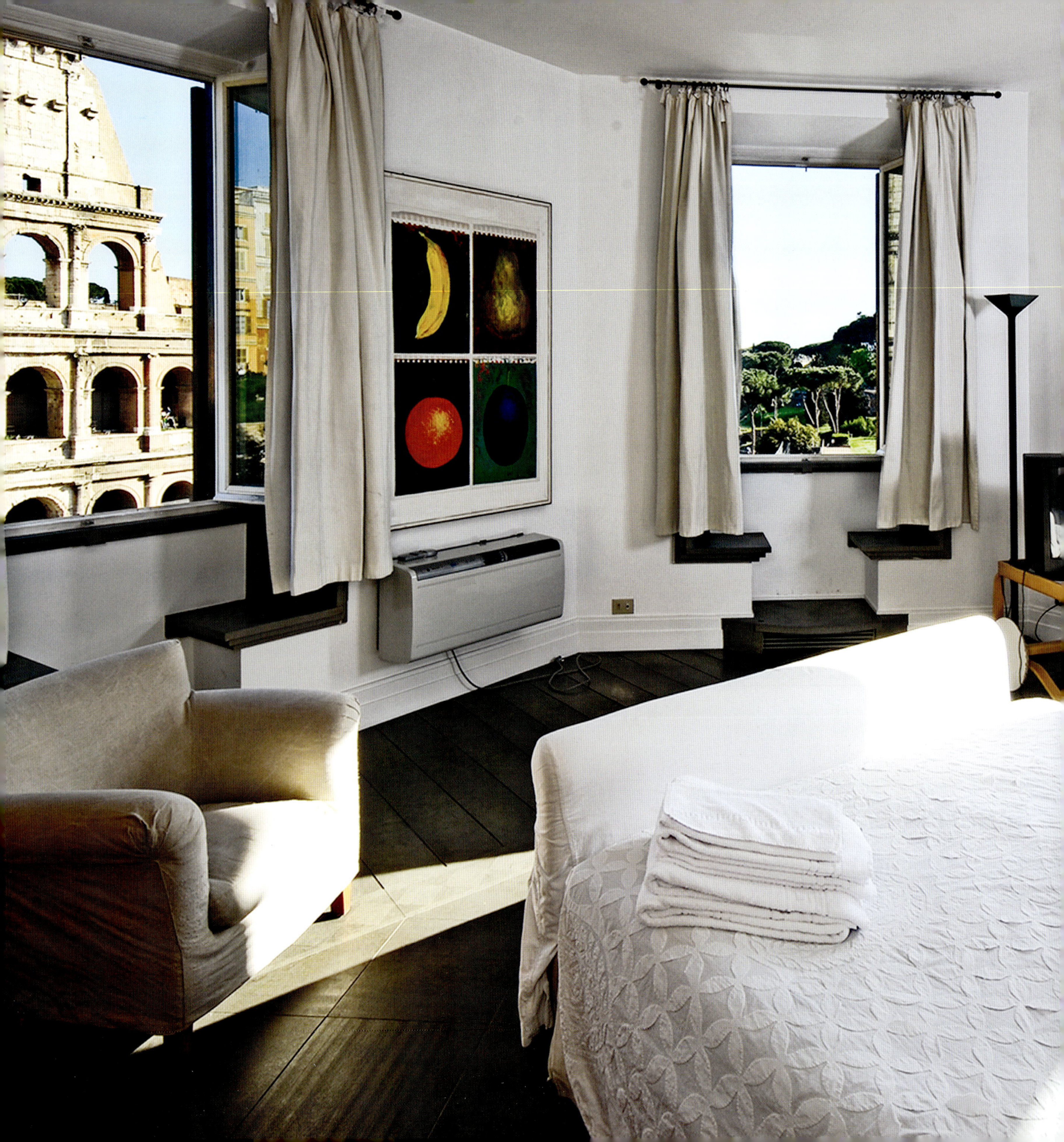

2014/15
CoolBrands.uk.com

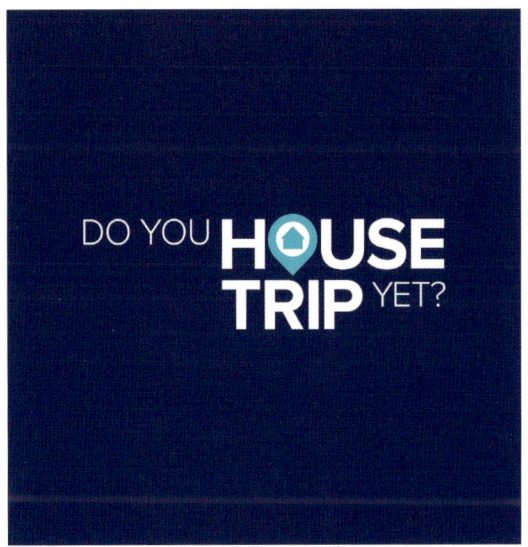

HouseTrip

The best place for families to find and book a whole home, apartment or villa for a holiday, HouseTrip is one of the largest holiday rental websites in the world.

Offering the comforts of an entire house, villa or apartment, but for less than the price of a hotel, to HouseTrip is to holiday without compromise. A HouseTrip stay means value, space, privacy, flexibility and the freedom to holiday on your own terms. With the best customer satisfaction scores in the whole travel industry, HouseTrip has been ranked as one of Europe's 100 hottest start-ups by Wired Magazine and as one of the 50 top websites for travel by The Times.

housetrip.com

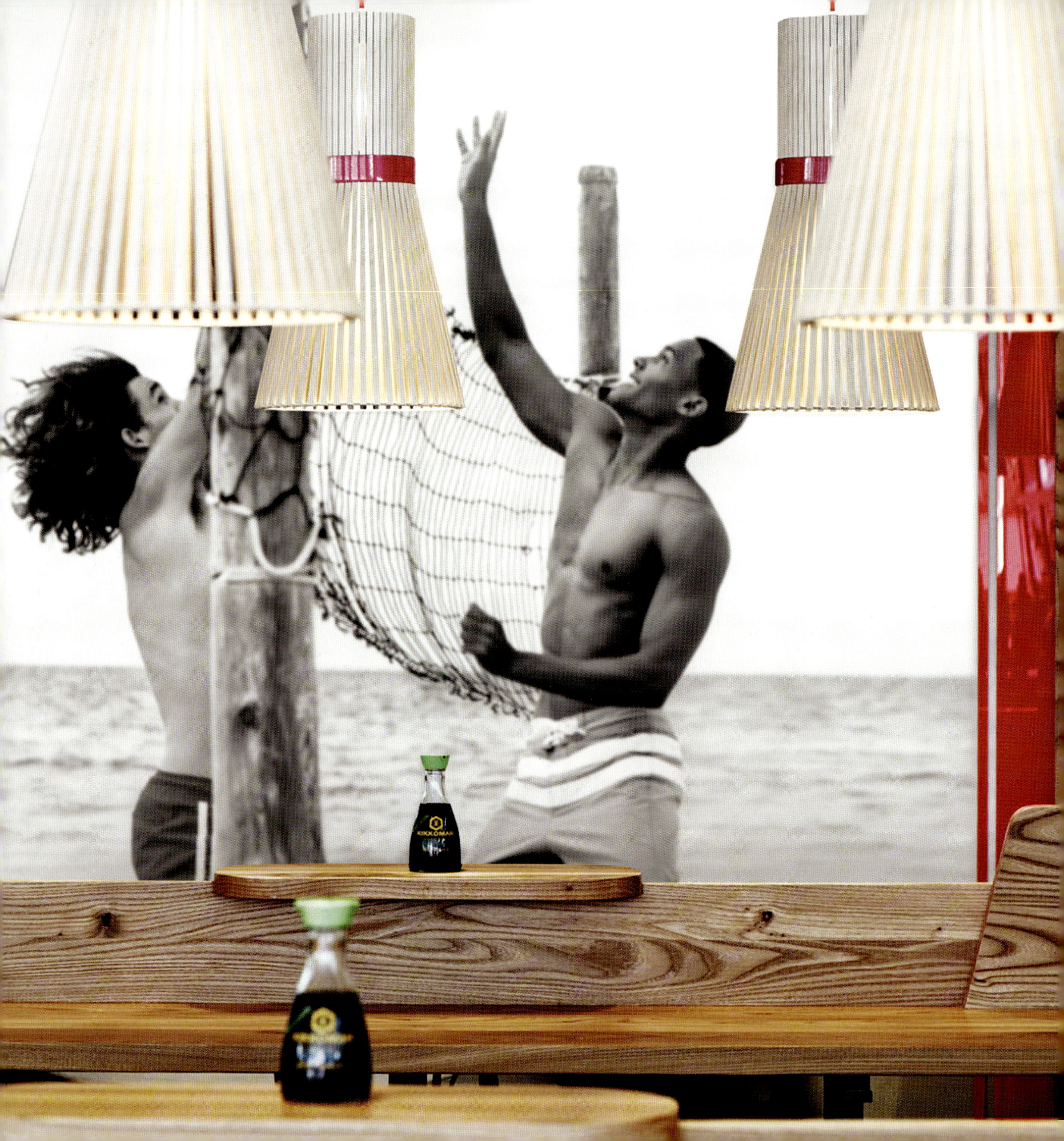
KIKKOMAN

2014/15
CoolBrands.uk.com

itsu

There are two flagship itsu restaurants and 60 dynamic shops – some with 100 seats, some with 10. Starting in Chelsea in 1997, the brand is growing fast.

The early pioneers of Pret are the creative force behind itsu. Years of listening to customers persuaded them to create itsu – a new type of place dedicated to lower fat, lower calorie, delicious food. Its purpose: to help people eat beautiful. No more same old gloom and gloop but days powered by butterfly light, wonderful flavours; protein packed, low carbohydrate, green and good for you. Hot or cold, in or out, home and away, early or late.

itsu.com

itsu
eat beautiful

JO
LOVES...
POMELO
A FRAGRANCE
30 ml e
1 fl oz/OZ LIQ
JO
LOVES...
PINK VETIVER
A FRAGRANCE
30 ml e
1 fl oz/OZ LIQ
JO
LOVES...
WILD RESEDA
A SCENTED CANDLE
JO
LOVES...
GREEN ORANGE
& CORIANDER
A BATH COLOGNE
200 ml e
6.8 fl oz/OZ LIQ

JO LOVES

Created by Jo Malone MBE, the JO LOVES brand bottles Jo's undeniable passion for fragrance, pouring undiluted creativity into innovative new products and entertaining experiences.

Jo Malone MBE – renowned scent maverick and the woman responsible for creating some of the world's most-loved fragrances – is changing the way we experience fragrance for a second time. Following her departure from the brand eponymous with her name, Jo's passion for fragrance never ceased and after much anticipation, JO LOVES was unveiled. Inspired by moments in life that make Jo's heart beat, the JO LOVES collection comes alive at the Elizabeth Street Fragrance Brasserie Bar.

joloves.com

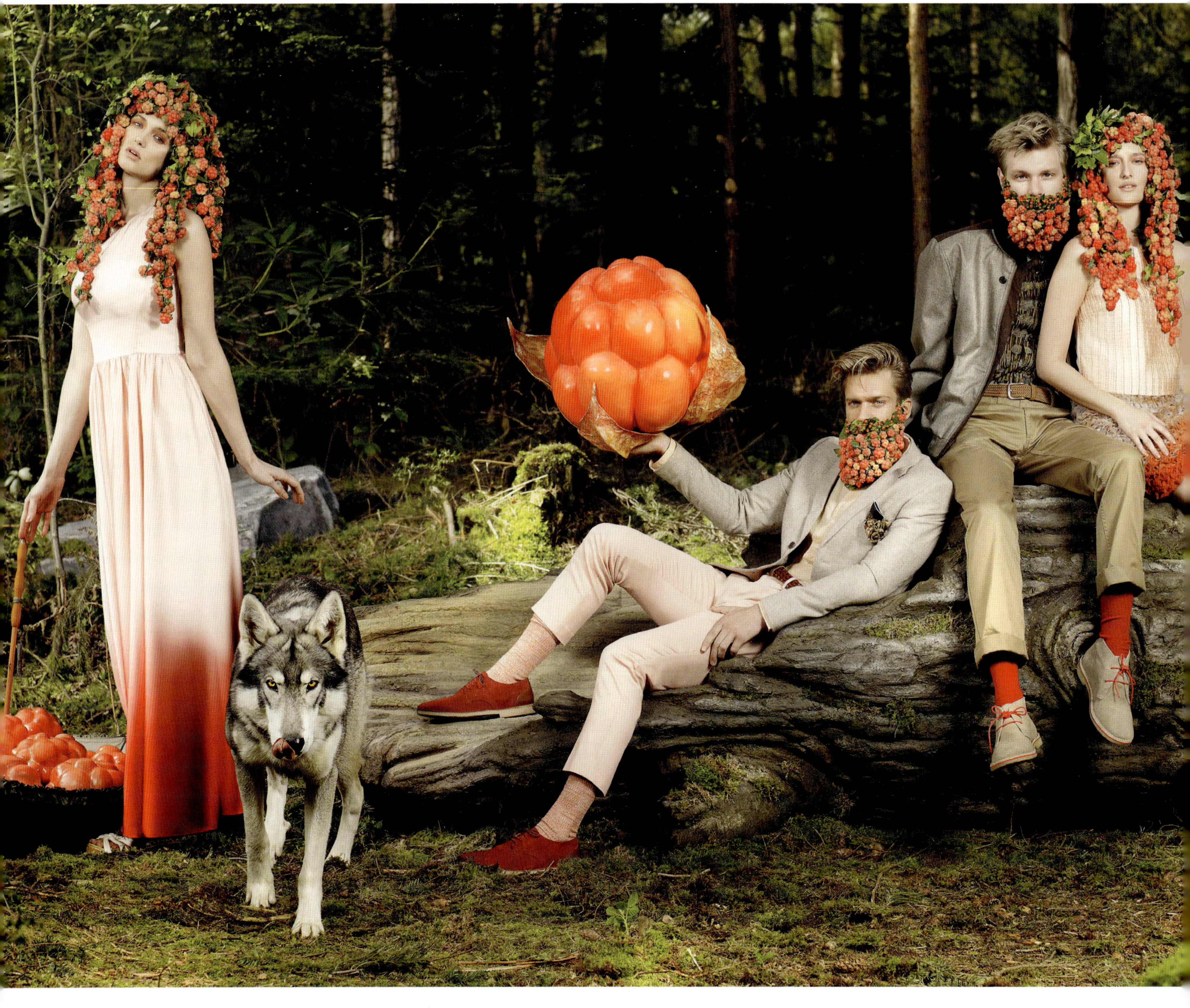

2014/15
CoolBrands.uk.com

Kopparberg

The pioneer of fruit cider, Kopparberg arrived from Sweden eight years ago and has become the UK's favourite premium cider brand.

Tucked away in a forest, four hours from Stockholm, is the small town of Kopparberg. It's not easy to get to, but this beautiful place is a hive of activity because it's where the world's best-selling fruit cider is made. The Kopparbergs Bryggeri was first built over 130 years ago and is today owned by the Bronsman family. Scandi, cool and very tasty, Kopparberg leads the fruit cider revolution from the front.

kopparberg.co.uk

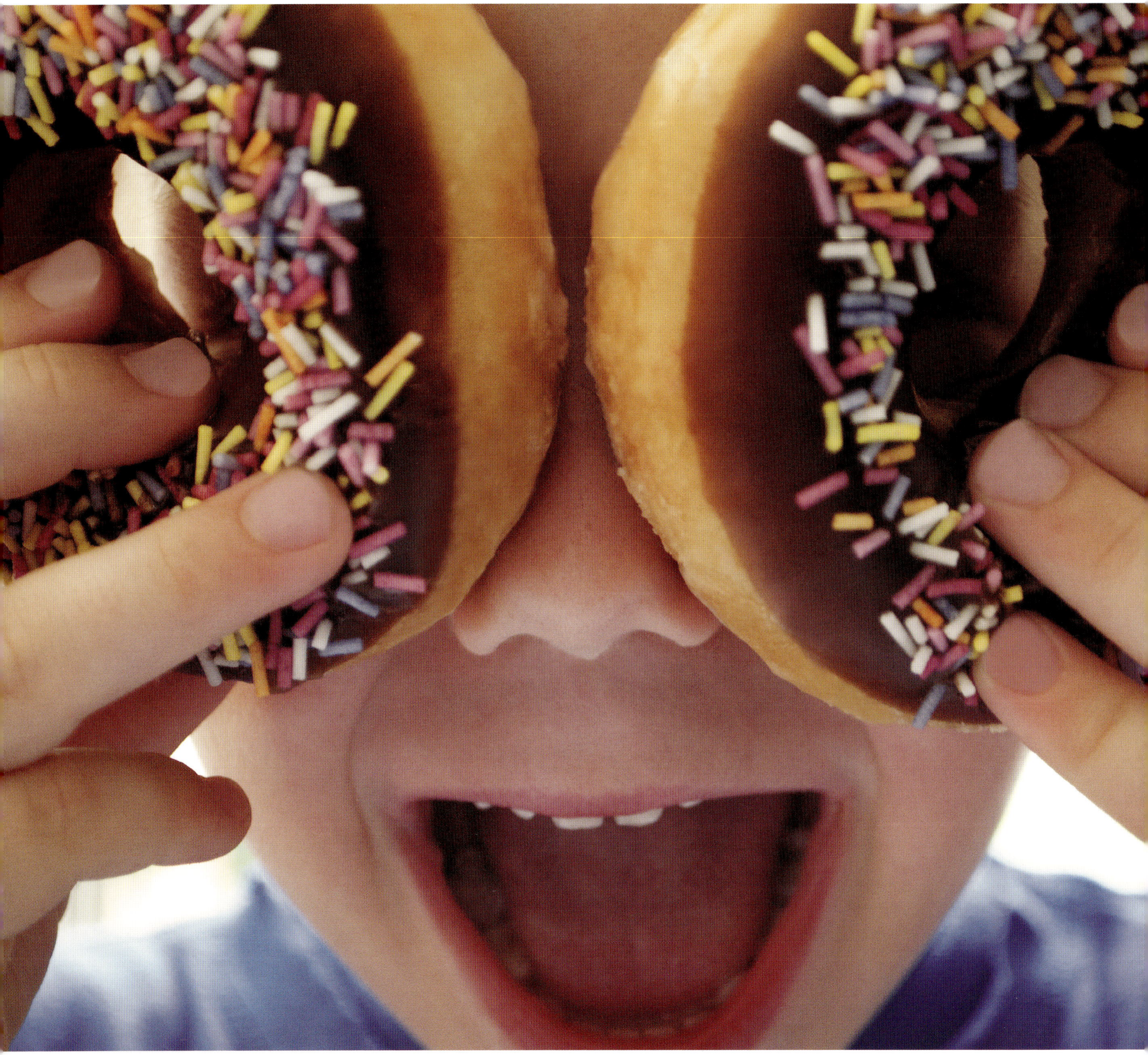

2014/15
CoolBrands.uk.com

Krispy Kreme

Founded by Vernon Rudolph in 1937, Krispy Kreme's iconic sweet treats are now distributed globally, bringing delectable doughnuts into homes and offices worldwide.

Krispy Kreme has something to offer everyone, from its mouthwatering signature Original Glazed doughnuts to its 15 other delicious varieties, including Strawberries & Kreme, Lemon Meringue Pie and Chocolate Dreamcake. Traditionally bought by the dozen to share with friends, family and colleagues, Krispy Kreme doughnuts are presented to the world in the now iconic green dotted box, inspiring envy wherever they go.

krispykreme.co.uk

Laurent-Perrier
CUVÉE ROSÉ
CHAMPAGNE
Laurent-Perrier
MAISON FONDÉE
1812
BRUT

2014/15
CoolBrands.uk.com

Laurent-Perrier

Established in 1812, Champagne Laurent-Perrier has a pedigree for innovation, handcrafting a diverse and pioneering range of fine champagnes that are produced to traditional, time-honoured methods.

One of the most distinguished family-owned Champagne Houses, Laurent-Perrier was acquired by the Nonancourt family in 1949. In 1959, the House introduced the first multi-vintage prestige cuvée – Grand Siècle by Laurent-Perrier – and drove the evolution of the rosé category, launching Laurent-Perrier Cuvée Rosé in 1968. Laurent-Perrier has achieved 16 prestigious show gardens at The RHS Chelsea Flower Show as well as being the official champagne partner of Taste Festivals, Wilderness and the London Restaurant Festival.

CHAMPAGNE
Laurent-Perrier
MAISON FONDÉE
1812

laurent-perrier.co.uk

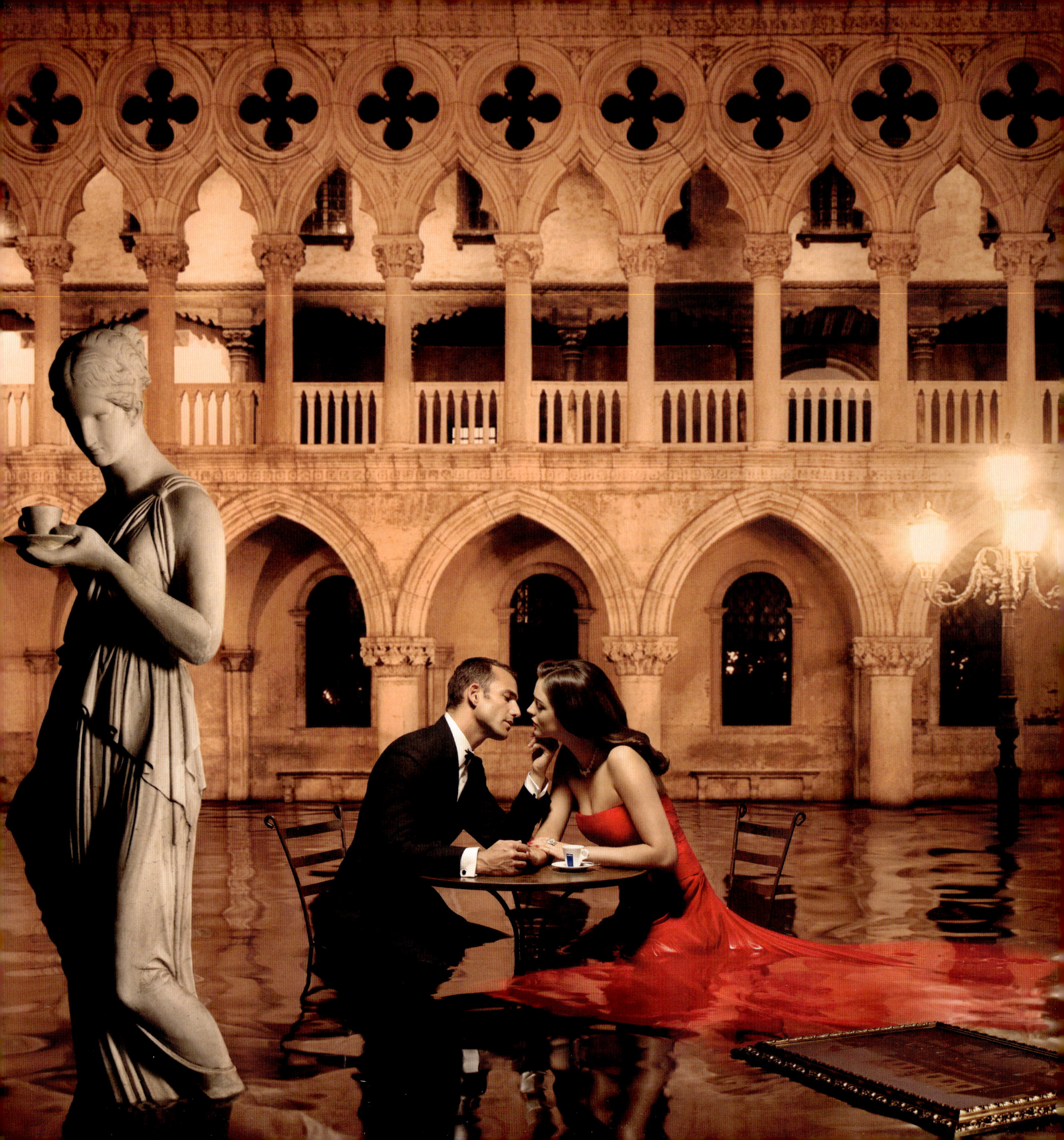

2014/15
CoolBrands.uk.com

Lavazza

Dedicating over 118 years of experience to create quality coffee blends, Lavazza is globally recognised as a symbol of authentic Italian espresso.

Lavazza's rich heritage is translated into its collection of fresh roast and ground blends, which are enjoyed by millions of food and drink lovers around the globe, both at home and in restaurants. Its innovative coffee machine range, A Modo Mio, adds style to any kitchen and creates perfect café quality coffees with ease. Espria, the newest machine in the range, fuses quality blends with the latest capsule technology to create espressos and Americanos with the touch of a button.

LAVAZZA
ITALY'S FAVOURITE COFFEE

lavazza.co.uk

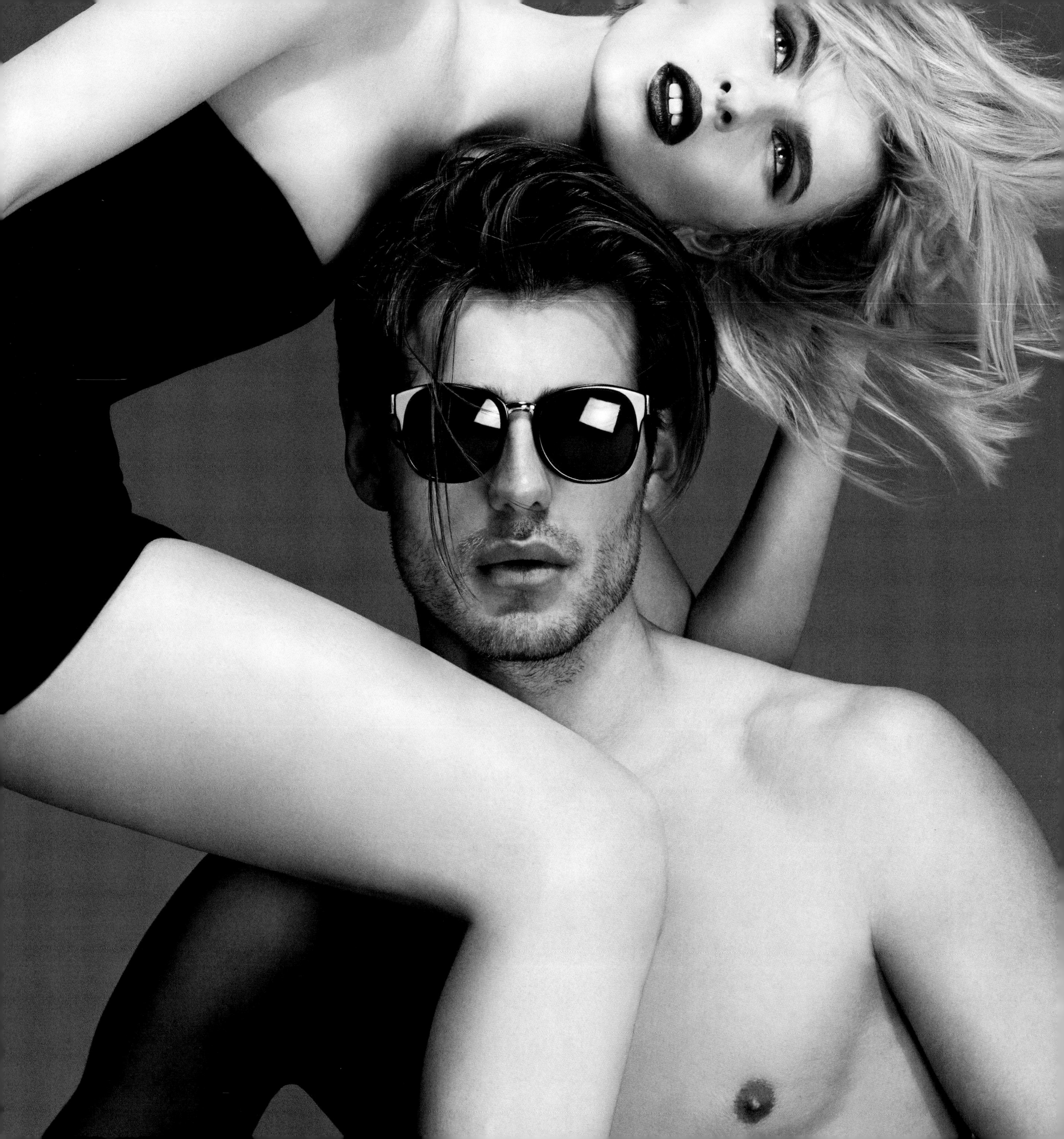

2014/15
CoolBrands.uk.com

Linda Farrow

Uncompromising in quality, unabashedly luxurious and timeless in design, Linda Farrow takes eyewear to the next level.

Synonymous with style, innovation, luxury and expertise within eyewear, Linda Farrow was relaunched ten years ago by her son, Simon Jablon, and Tracy Sedino. Treating eyewear as fashion, not a mere accessory, saw the brand collaborate with some of the most well-respected fashion designers under the Linda Farrow Gallery. Experimenting with materials, pushing the boundaries in design and maintaining the highest standard of production has established Linda Farrow as one of the most exciting brands in fashion today.

lindafarrow.com

LINDA FARROW

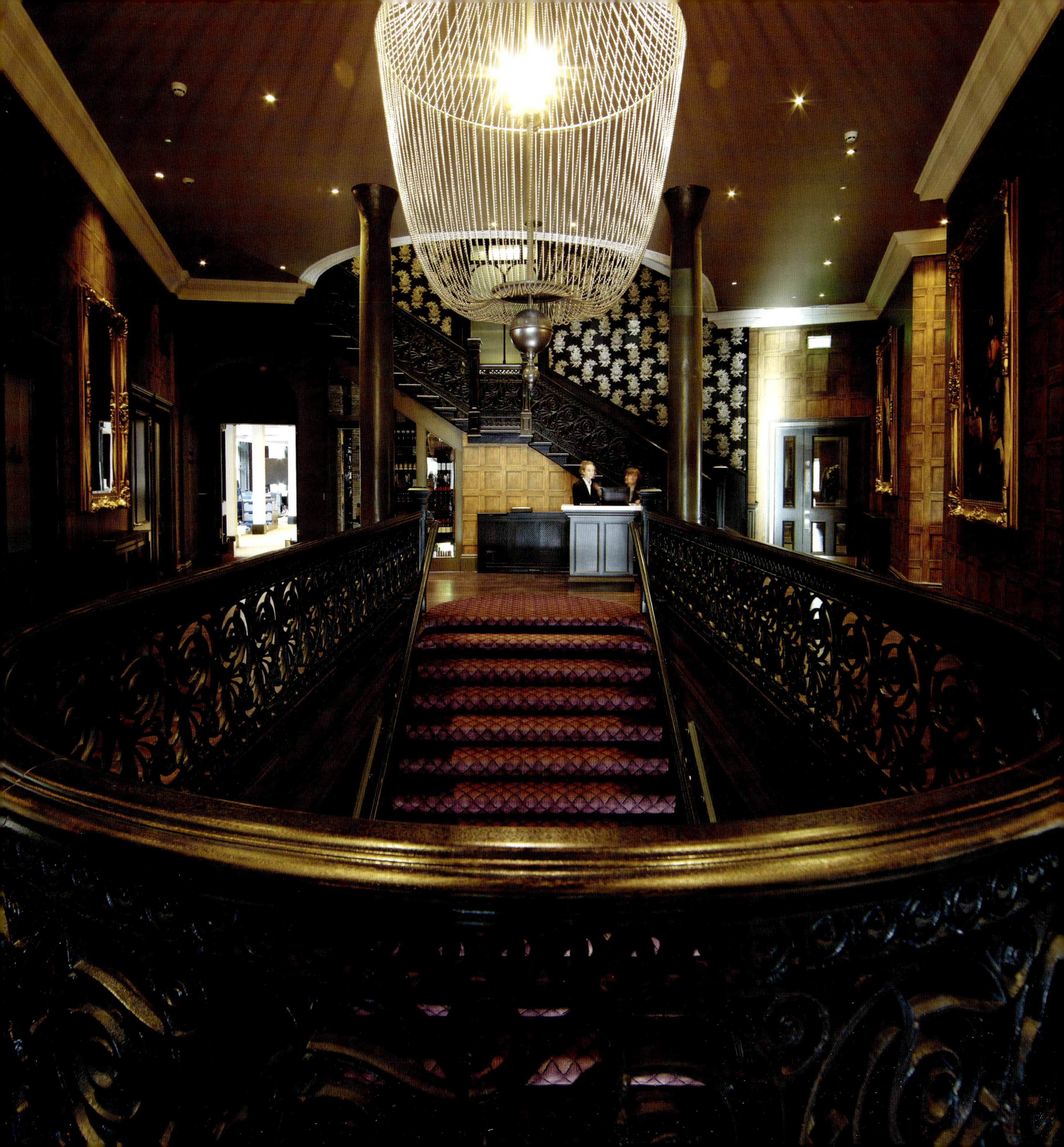

2014/15
CoolBrands.uk.com

Malmaison

An exciting and aspirational lifestyle brand, Malmaison continues to push the boundaries of quality, energy and creativity expected from boutique hotels and brasseries.

Malmaison exists to cater for those who demand something different; people who are looking for a stylish stay, daring dining or a truly impressive events venue with a rich, relaxed atmosphere. Each location is designed with flair and imagination, with sumptuous accommodation and energetic bars and brasseries in settings that look good enough to eat. In 2014, the stunningly restored Dundee and renovated apartment-feel London are new examples of the exciting, innovative conversions the brand is famous for.

malmaison.com

Malmaison
HOTELS
dare to be different

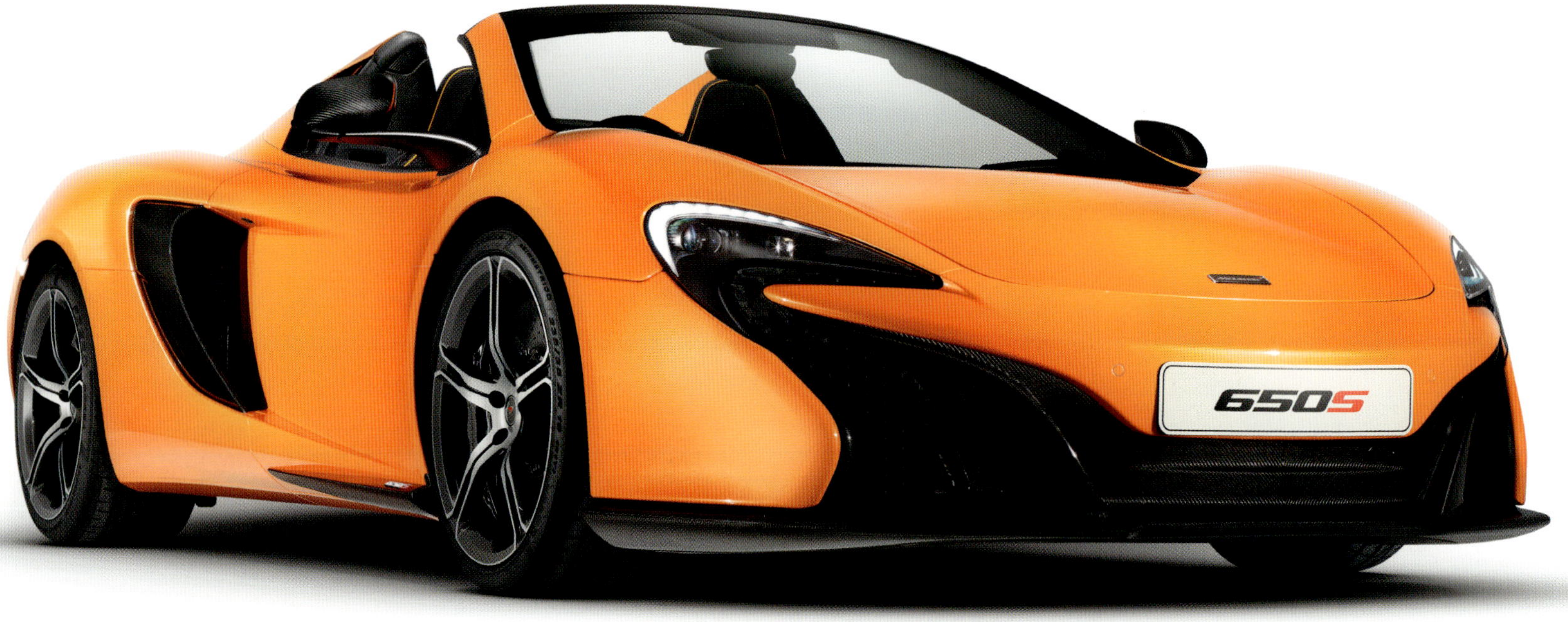
650S

2014/15
CoolBrands.uk.com

McLaren Automotive

One of Britain's most innovative brands, McLaren Automotive is bringing a new thrill and level of driver engagement to the luxury automotive market.

McLaren is now established as a benchmark in the automotive industry, achieving success on and off the track. The 12C was first in a new line-up of McLaren road cars, transferring Formula 1™ technology to the road, followed by the incredible sold-out McLaren P1™, one of the most technologically advanced hypercars ever manufactured. Building on five decades of expertise at the pinnacle of motorsport, McLaren has introduced the groundbreaking 650S, its most engaging and refined supercar to date.

cars.mclaren.com

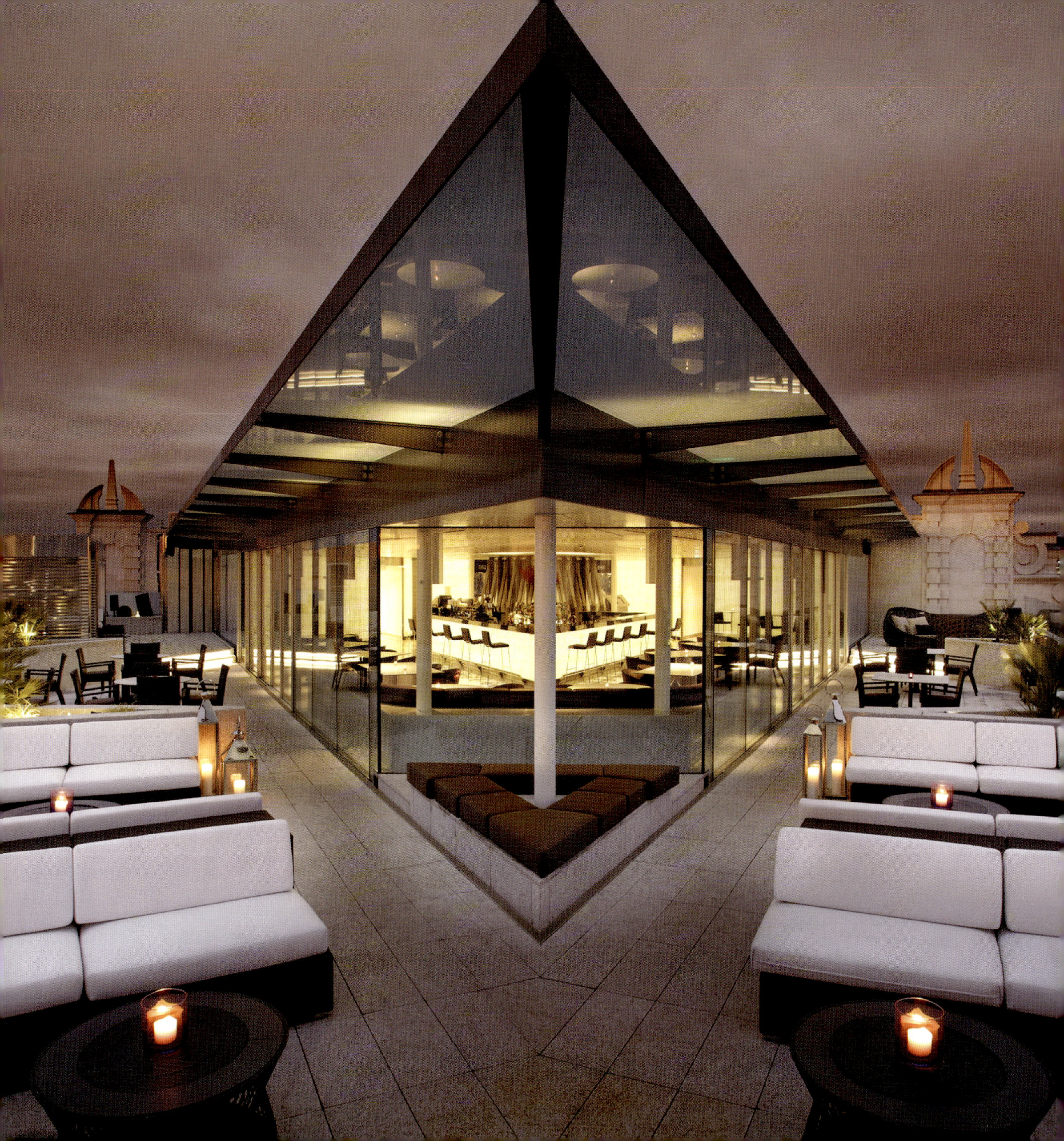

ME London

Established in 2006, ME London is the flagship property for the ME by Meliá group, offering 157 rooms with interiors that fuse contemporary detailing and classic traditions.

Fusing innovative style with local tastes in order to captivate travellers with a taste for cutting-edge art and design, international cuisine and world music, ME London is situated in the heart of London's Theatre district. Built on first-rate service, the hotel is the first flagship property in which everything, from the shell of the building to the bathroom fittings, has been designed by Foster + Partners. There are currently ME Hotels in London, Madrid, Cancun and Cabo.

melia.com

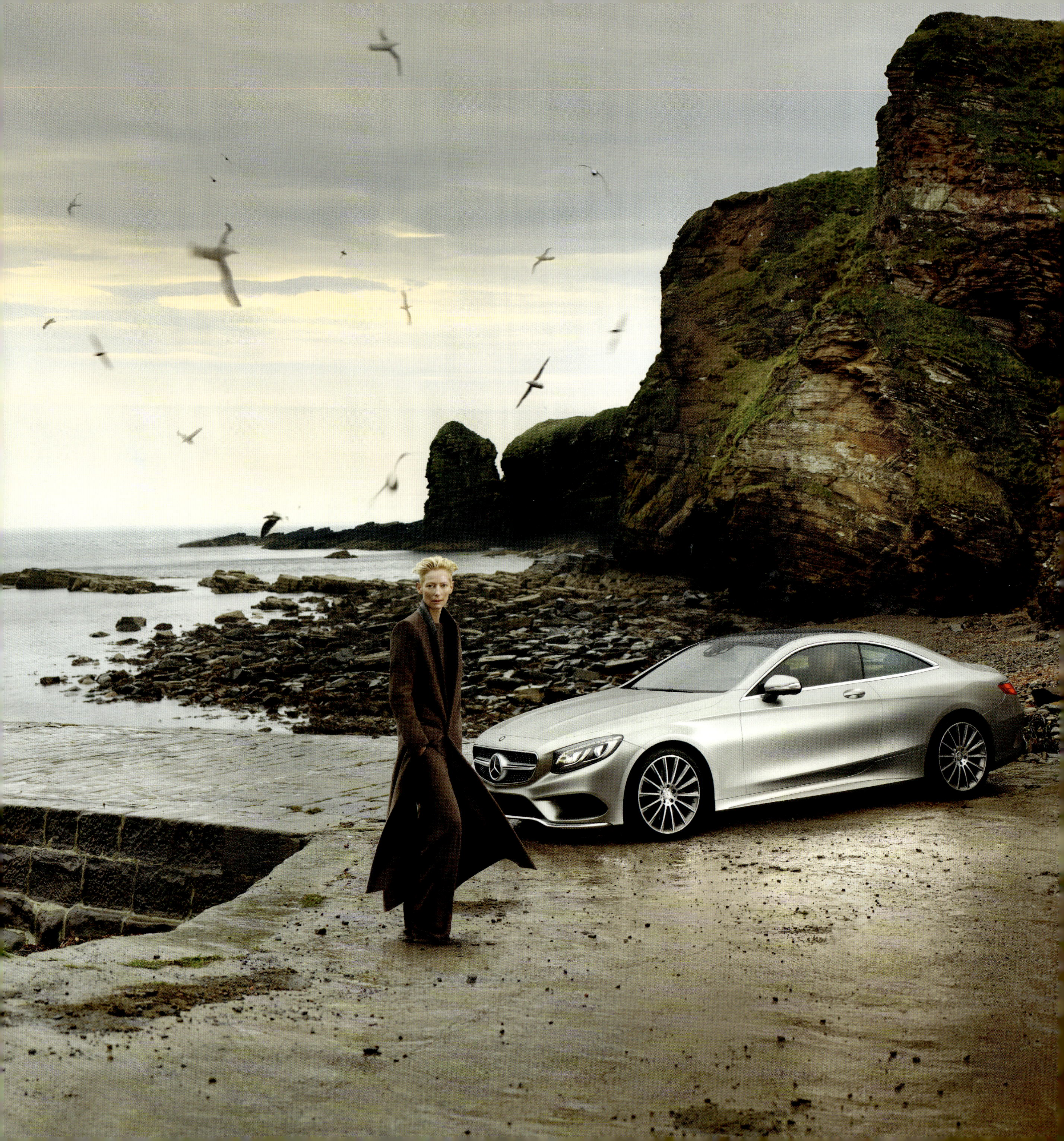

2014/15
CoolBrands.uk.com

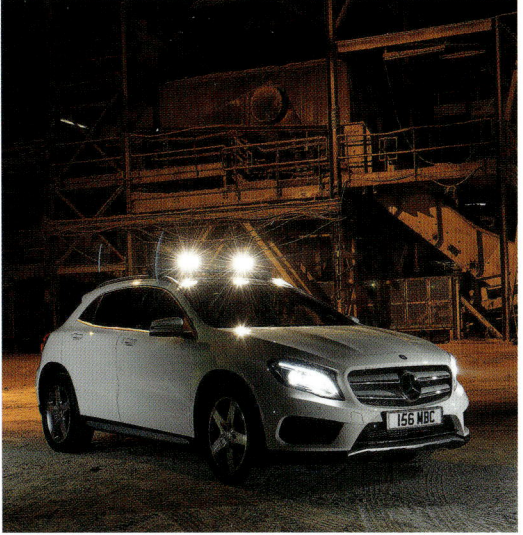

Mercedes-Benz

The iconic car brand that continues to forge new territory, Mercedes-Benz creates exciting, innovative products packed with advanced technology, and presented with effortless and ever-evolving style.

Mercedes-Benz is synonymous with style and glamour, yet the guiding principles in the creation of every car remain the same. Combining tradition with cutting-edge innovation, a stunning range of compact cars brings premium luxury to vibrant new audiences, making Mercedes-Benz even more relevant to more people. Whether it's building supercars or family cars, taking the chequered flag in Formula 1®, or supporting fashion events, Mercedes-Benz does things properly, with integrity, energy and style.

mercedes-benz.co.uk

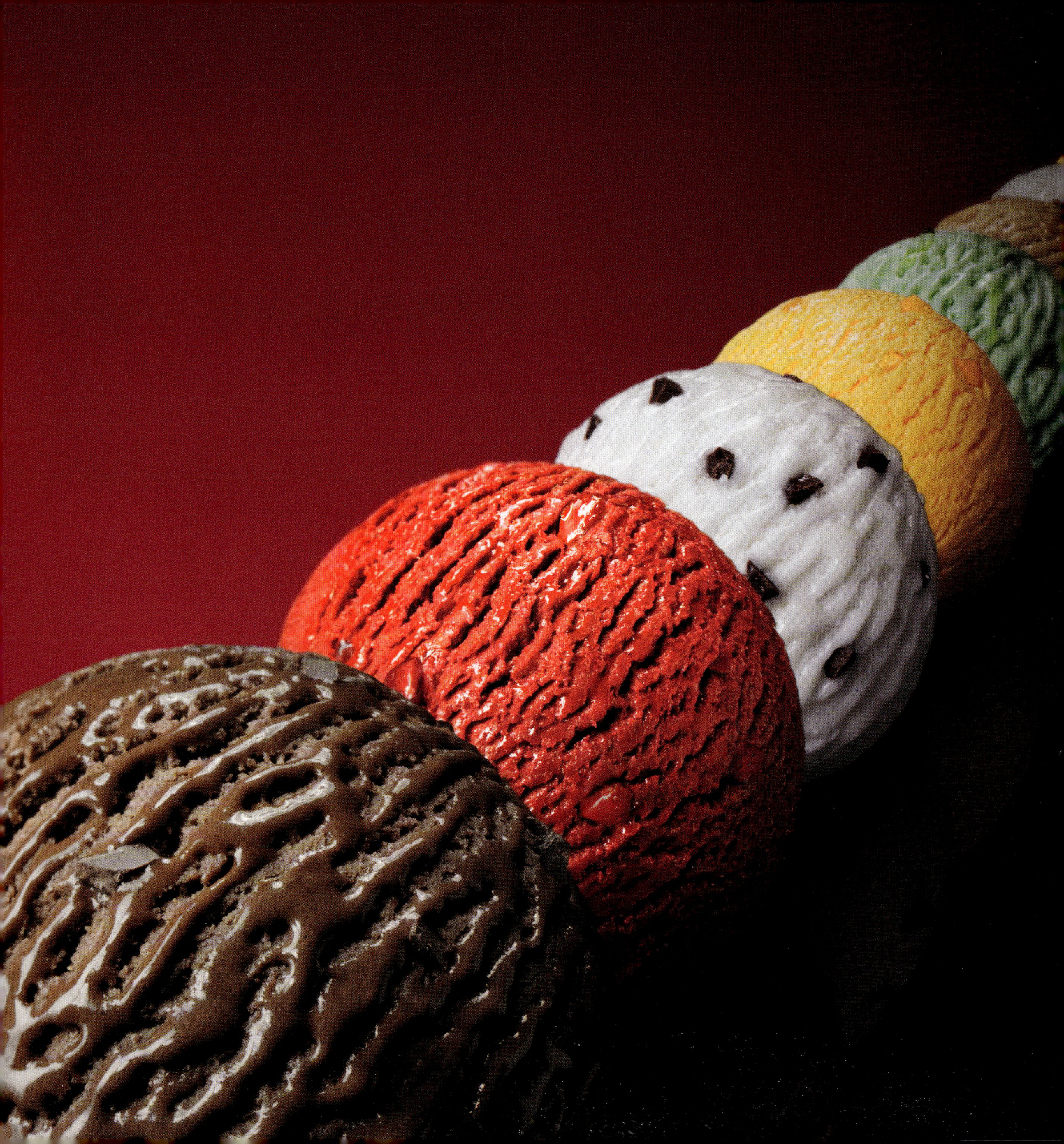

2014/15
CoolBrands.uk.com

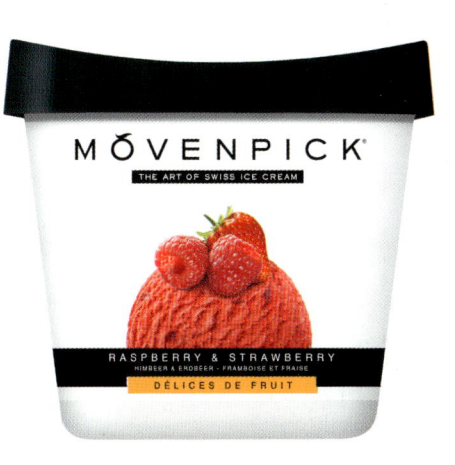

Mövenpick Ice Cream

Mövenpick Ice Cream owes its inspiration to a revolutionary vision of culinary excellence that swept through the kitchens of Swiss restaurants in the 1960s.

The Mövenpick Ice Cream Makers – or Maître Glaciers as they are often known – are the authors of every delicious recipe, creating luxurious ice cream that's consistent in quality and taste. The ice cream flavours are there to be discovered, whether filled with Bourbon vanilla from Madagascar, Maracaibo cocoa from Venezuela, handcrafted caramel or hand-picked raspberries of the Héritage variety. Mövenpick Ice Cream is authentic, never touching artificial additives, flavours or colours.

MÖVENPICK
THE ART OF SWISS ICE CREAM

moevenpick-icecream.co.uk

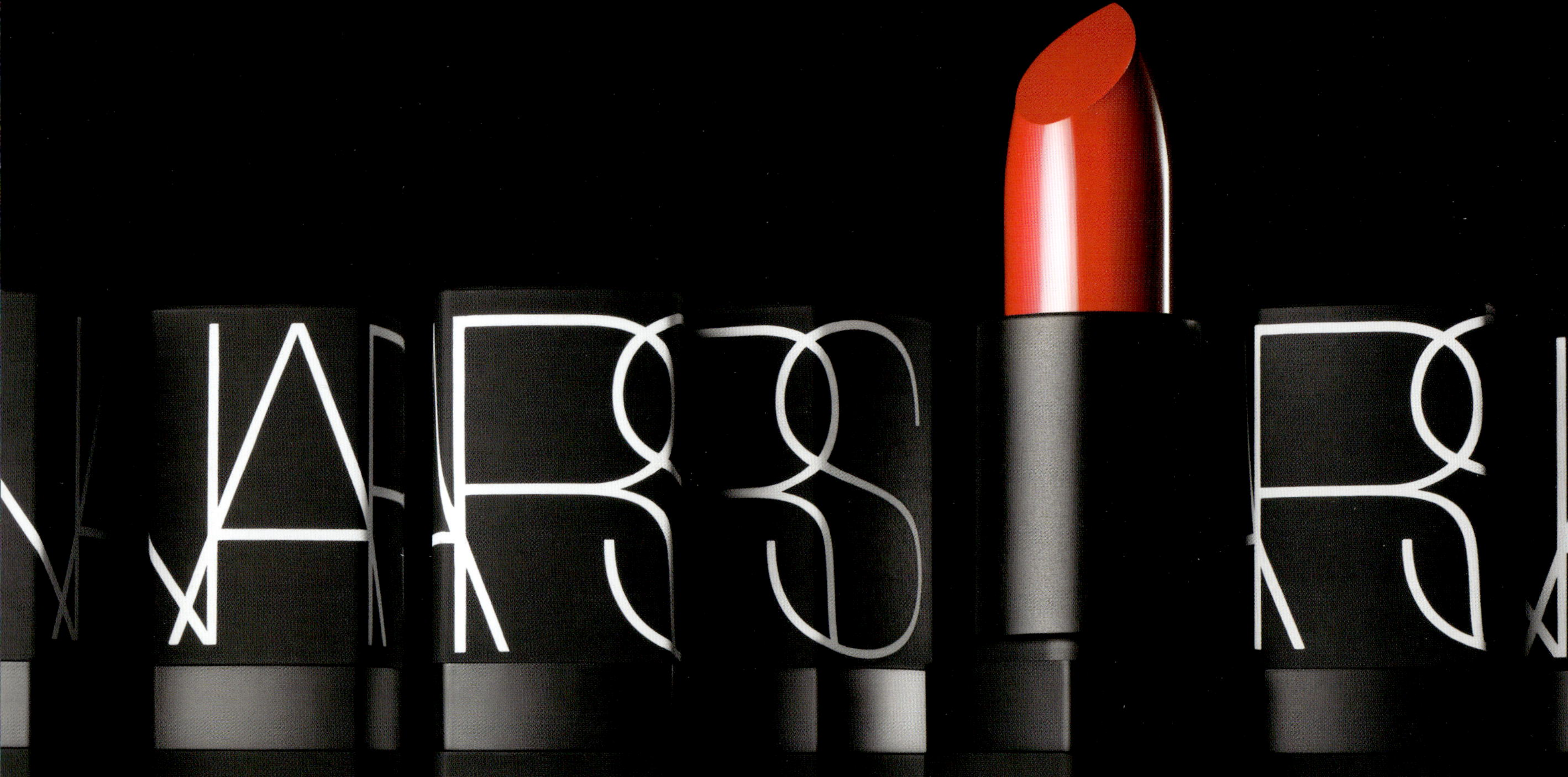

2014/15
CoolBrands.uk.com

NARS

Modern, audacious and iconic, NARS combines high style with pioneering beauty, underpinned by the words of Founder, François Nars, "Don't be so serious; it's only makeup!"

Makeup artist. Photographer. Iconoclast. François Nars is one of the most influential image-makers in the world. His rule-breaking philosophy of beauty celebrates bold originality, supporting decades of fashion world collaborations with designers such as Marc Jacobs and Karl Lagerfeld. The brand, born of François' fascination with colour purity, debuted with 12 original high-pigment lipsticks at Barney's New York. Twenty years and countless collections later, NARS continues to bring high fashion, high style, and forward thinking to beauty.

NARS

narscosmetics.co.uk

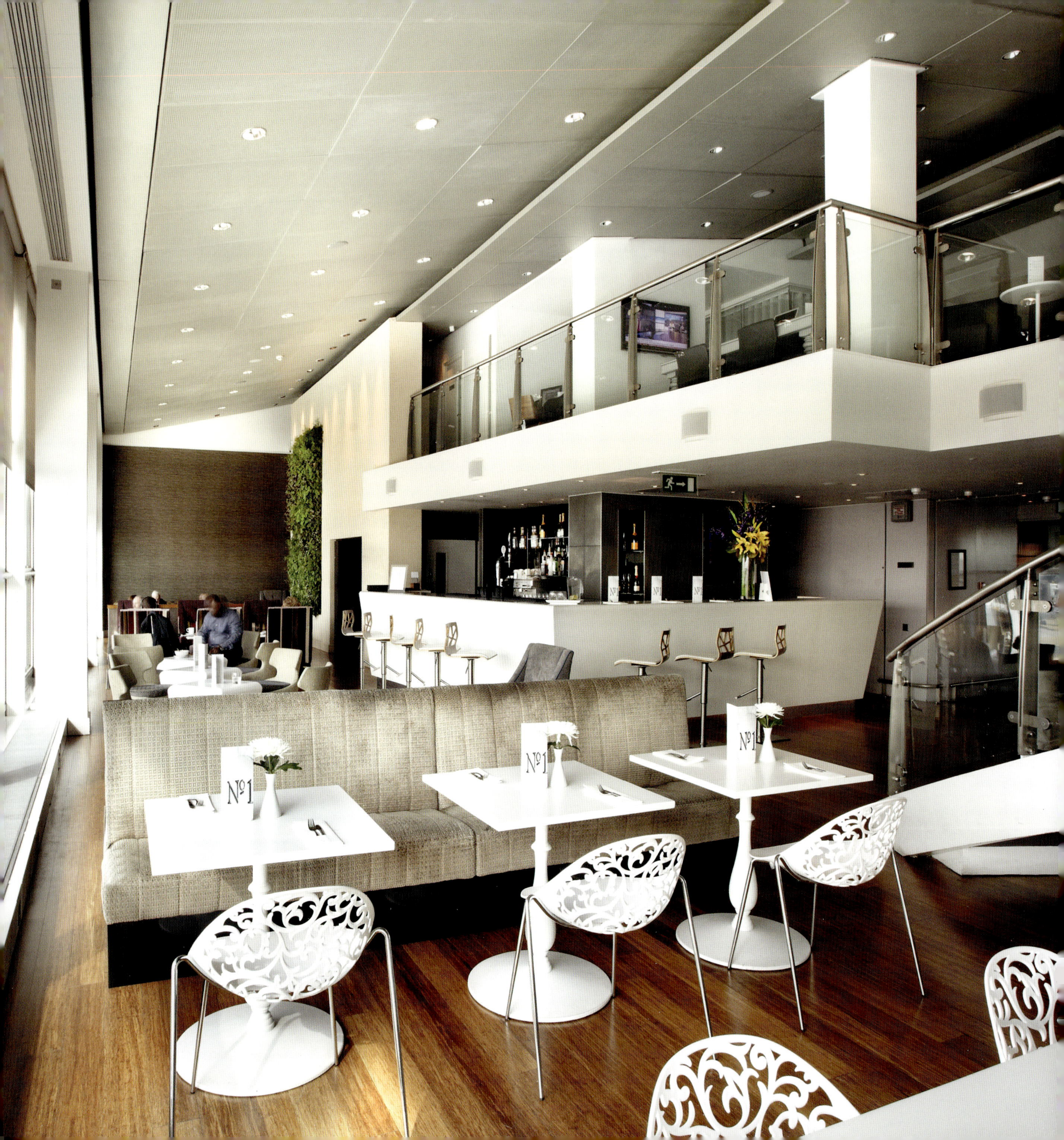
№1
№1
№1

2014/15
CoolBrands.uk.com

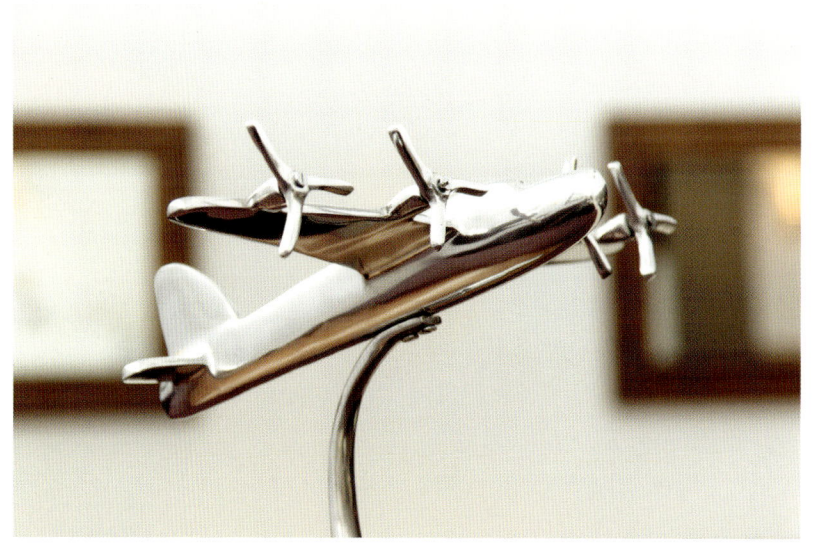

No.1 Lounges

No.1 Lounges leads the way in putting the jet set back into catching a flight, with an award-winning collection of airport lounges and travel spas.

Even in the most impressive new terminals, there will always be bustle, queues and waiting around. Where's the glamour gone? With No.1 Lounges, arrive at the airport with a private chauffeur, get whisked through the terminal and make the hours before a flight about chilled wines, soothing massages and time well spent. Anyone can upgrade with No.1, regardless of destination or class of travel. The journey begins at No1Lounges.com and continues at Heathrow, Gatwick, Stansted, Edinburgh or Birmingham.

No.1 LOUNGES

no1lounges.com

YOUR SLOGAN HERE
TELEPHONE
FOR RENT
INQUIRE
LONDON
UNITED KINGDOM
REPUBLIC OF IRELAND

2014/15
CoolBrands.uk.com

Pedlars

Selling wonderful homewares, bags, stationery and gifts, Pedlars' varied stock ranges from pieces produced here in Britain to vintage items from across the globe.

A family-run business based in North Wales with a general store and café in Notting Hill, Pedlars offers a curated, considered and beautifully designed range of homewares and gifts. Interested in products with stories to tell, with patina, history and a good dose of warmth and fun, the now well-established Pedlars Friday Vintage initiative sees the brand working with a network of dealers to create weekly parcels of best-quality vintage items for the home and garden.

pedlars.co.uk

PEDLARS

TRICHOTHERAPY®

2014/15
CoolBrands.uk.com

Philip Kingsley

Philip Kingsley adopts a holistic approach to hair care, encompassing a regular hair and scalp regime and optimum nutrition, to ensure every day is a happy hair day.

Formulated by the world's leading hair and scalp experts, Philip Kingsley is dedicated to creating products that make your hair healthy and beautiful. With over 60 years of trichological experience, an impressive celebrity following and an award-winning product range, this year Philip Kingsley introduces Trichotherapy® – a unique and revolutionary hair and scalp regime that offers the ultimate solution for fine, thinning hair.

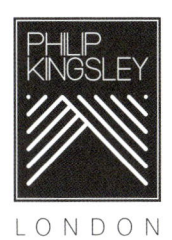

philipkingsley.co.uk

PHILIP KINGSLEY
LONDON

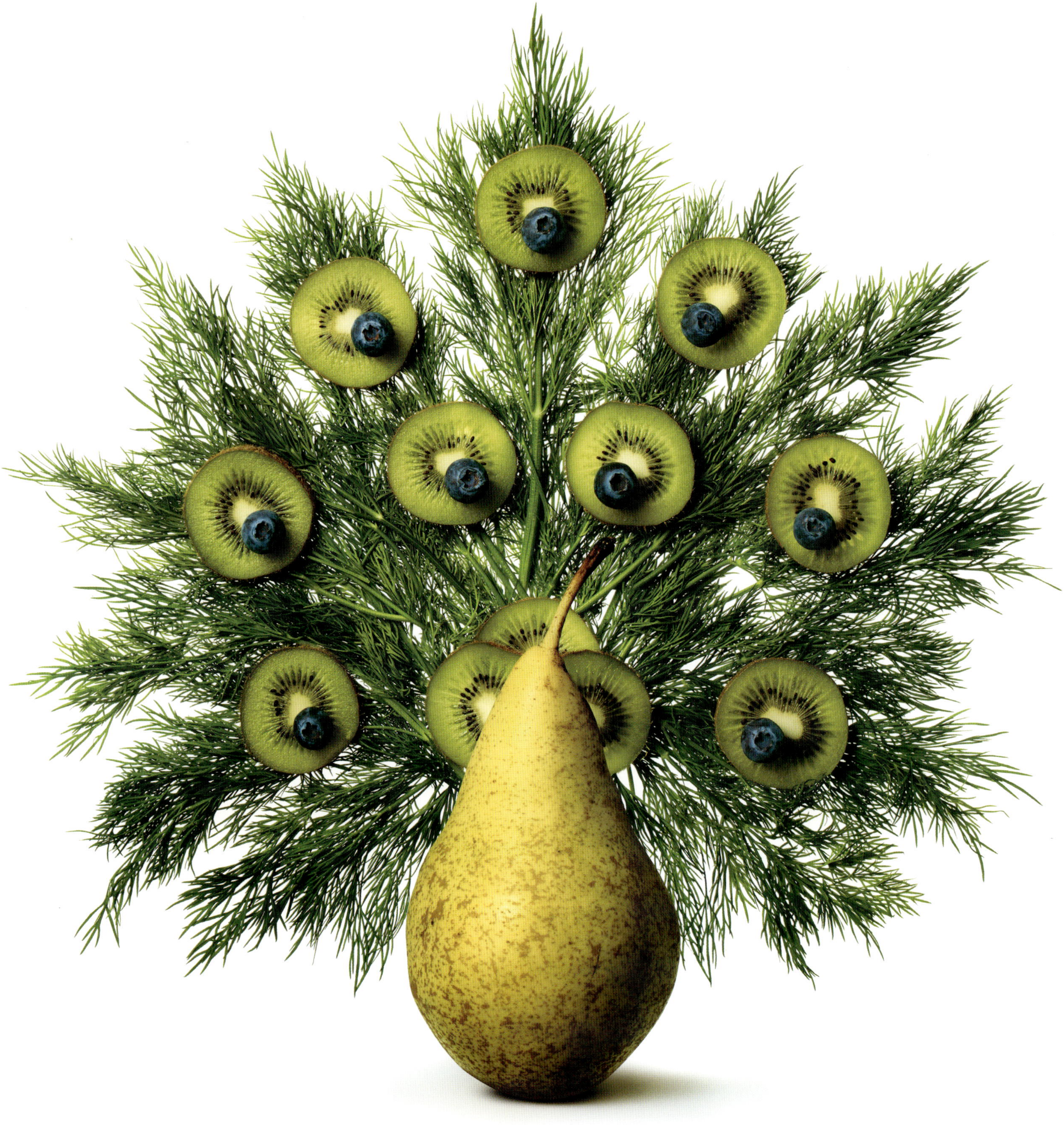

2014/15
CoolBrands.uk.com

Pret A Manger

Creating natural food and organic coffee, Pret A Manger avoids the obscure chemicals, preservatives and additives found in many 'prepared' and 'fast' foods on the market today.

Dedicated to handmade, freshly prepared food since 1986, Pret's kitchens are stocked every morning with ethically sourced, natural ingredients. That same passion gets poured into every cup of its organic coffee; Pret travels around the world to meet coffee farmers, building long-term relationships and sharing knowledge that supports sustainable farming practices. This means that its brilliant baristas work with only the best organic beans, freshly roasted and served in over 350 stores around the world.

pret.com

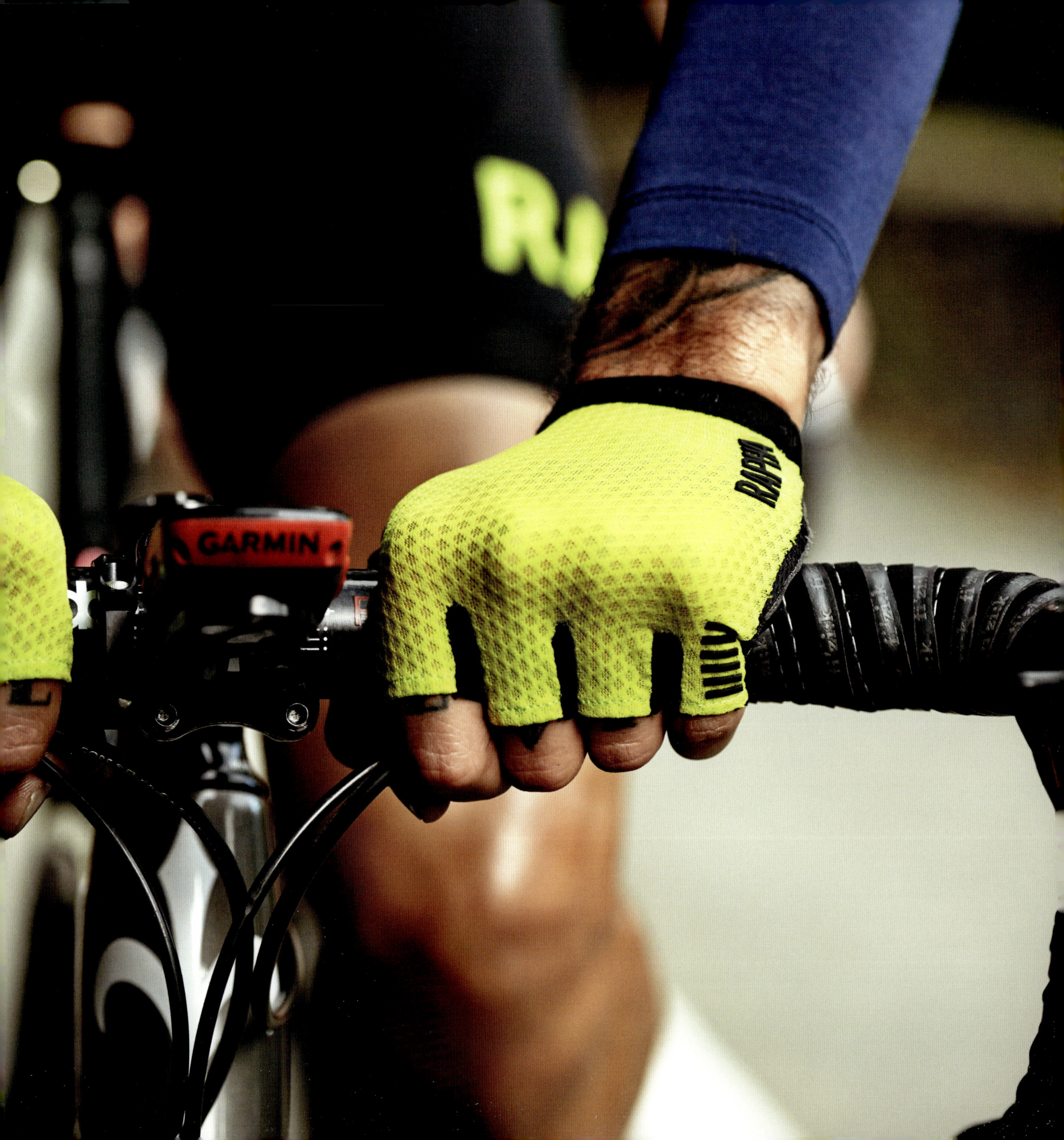
GARMIN
RAPHA

2014/15
CoolBrands.uk.com

Rapha

Designed without compromise for the most discerning rider, Rapha products blend optimum performance and modern style to create the finest cycling clothing and accessories in the world.

A passion for road racing means Rapha is more than just a product company; it is an online emporium of performance roadwear, accessories, publications and events, all celebrating the glory and suffering of road riding. Launched in 2004 with just a handful of products, Rapha has gone on to organise rides, races and events, make films, produce books and sponsor three professional teams. In 2013, it became official clothing sponsor to Team Sky Pro Cycling.

rapha.cc

Rapha®

REKORDERLIG
REKORDERLIG
STRAWBERRY-LIME
PREMIUM CIDER
4.0

2014/15
CoolBrands.uk.com

Rekorderlig

Enjoyed by those who yearn for something refreshingly different, Rekorderlig invites drinkers on a journey of exploration, innovation and invigoration.

From its humble Swedish roots, Rekorderlig has retained its dependable honesty to become a much-loved, fourth generation family-made cider – a reliable and premium cider to rely on and trust. With a typically Swedish fusion of high-end, premium design and modesty, it has a clear identity that sets it apart from others and continues to launch in new countries while maintaining its proud Swedish heritage.

REKORDERLIG CIDER

rekorderlig.com

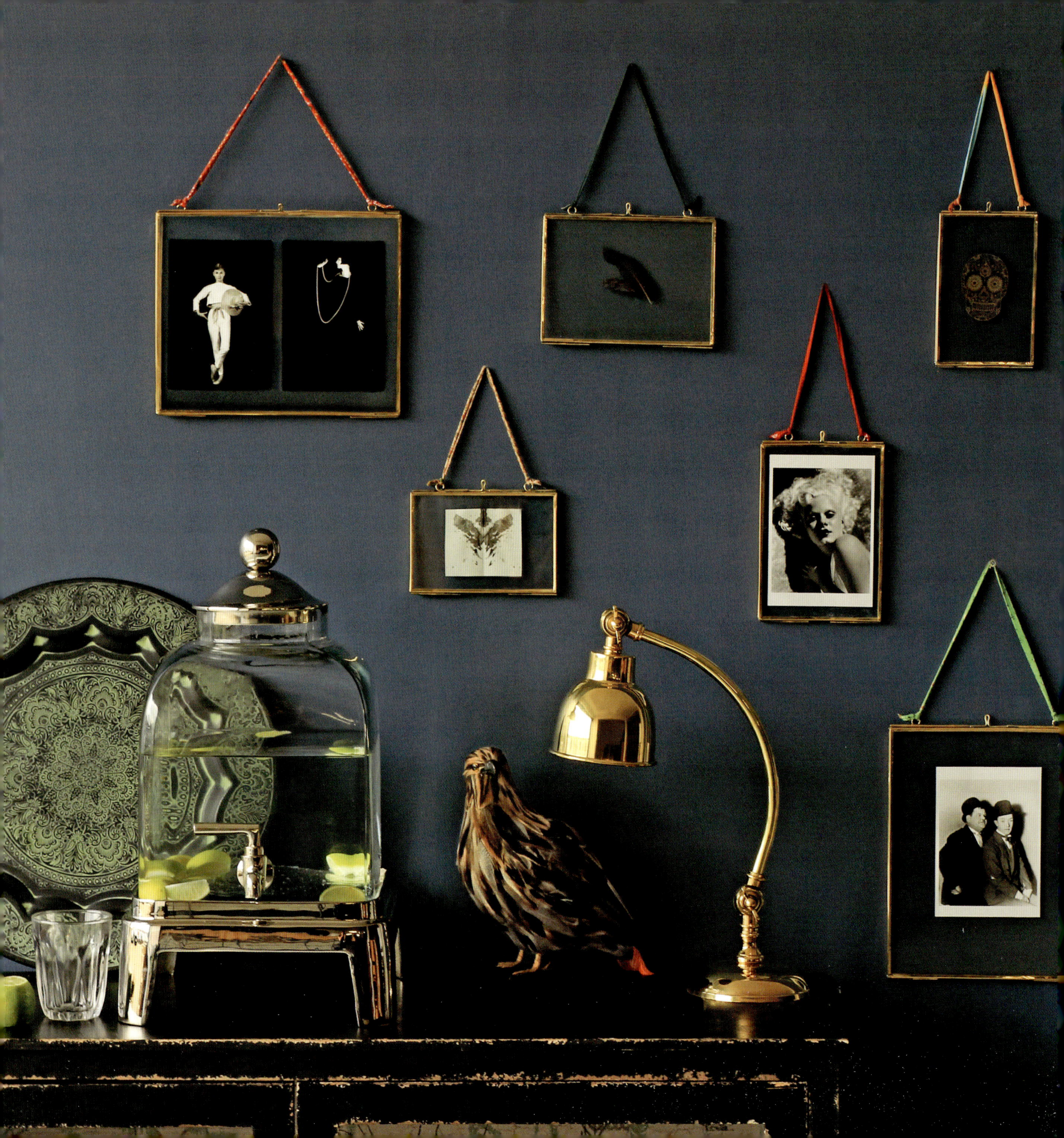

2014/15
CoolBrands.uk.com

Rockett St George

An online emporium of expressive homeware with an exceptionally quirky style, Rockett St George's eclectic mix of treasures inject magic, charm and personality into interiors.

Rockett St George has revitalised the interiors market by enabling customers to break free from chain store offerings and stamp personality on their homes. The online store is a treasure trove of oddities and curiosities collected from designers and manufacturers all around the world. Founders, Jane and Lucy, spend their time looking for inspiration and discovering new artists, designers and products. Its cleverly curated collections are a firm favourite of the press, interior designers and loyal customers.

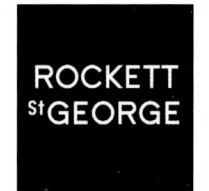

rockettstgeorge.co.uk

ROCKETT St GEORGE

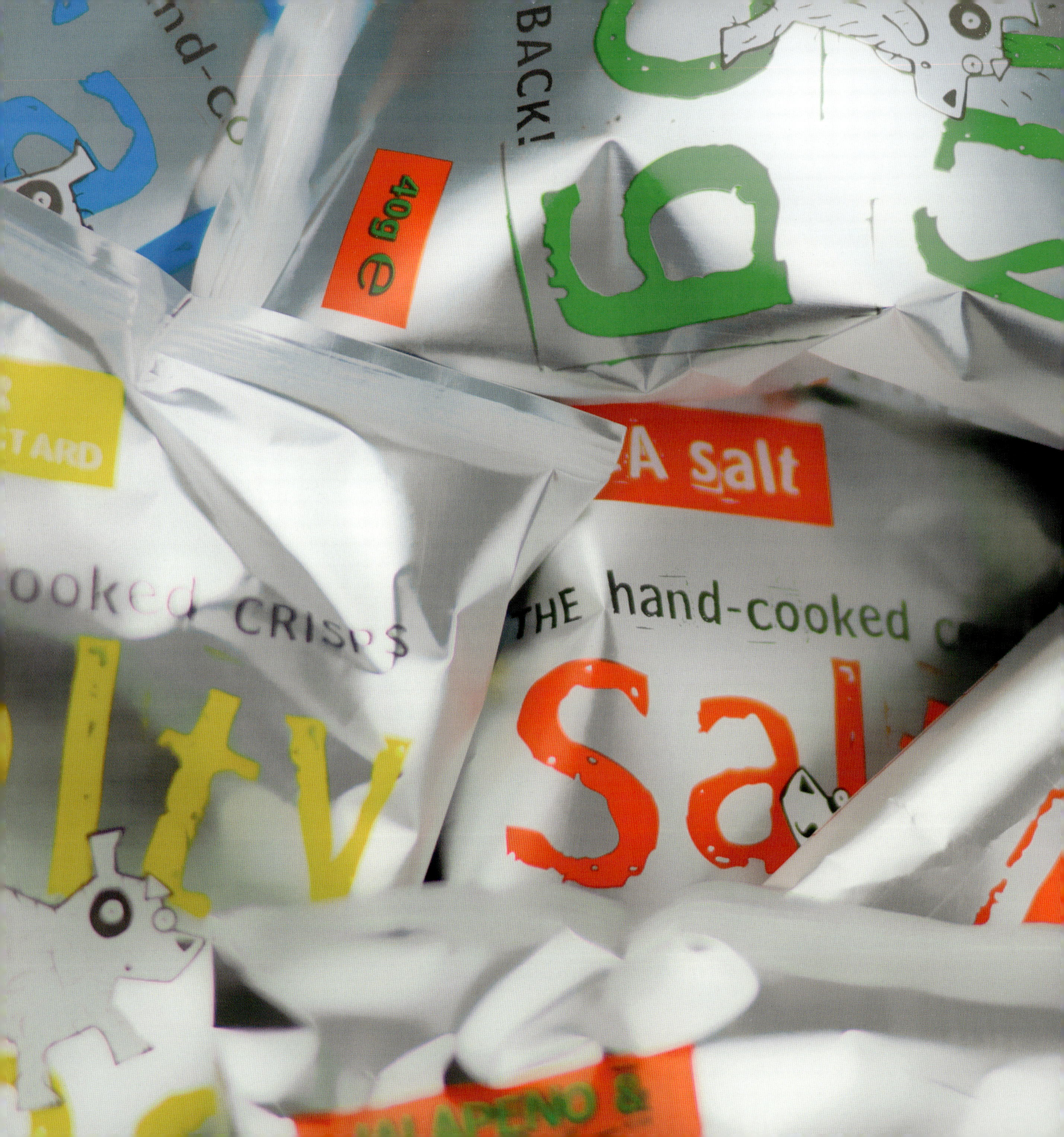
BACK!
40g e
A salt
ooked CRISPS
THE hand-cooked

2014/15
CoolBrands.uk.com

Salty Dog

Creating hand-cooked crisps with real bite, Salty Dog digs up only the finest potatoes, which are thickly sliced, seasoned with natural flavourings and cooked to crunchy perfection.

It is the extra love and care lavished on its potatoes that makes Salty Dog stand out from the crowd – after all, a pampered potato is a happy potato. The name a nod to the founders' trusty terrier puppy, Ruby, Salty Dog was created in 2003 by Judy and Dave Willis. A selection of delicious nuts and gourmet popcorn have since been added to the range, continuing in its mission to delight the nation with feisty, artisan snacks.

saltydog-grrr.com

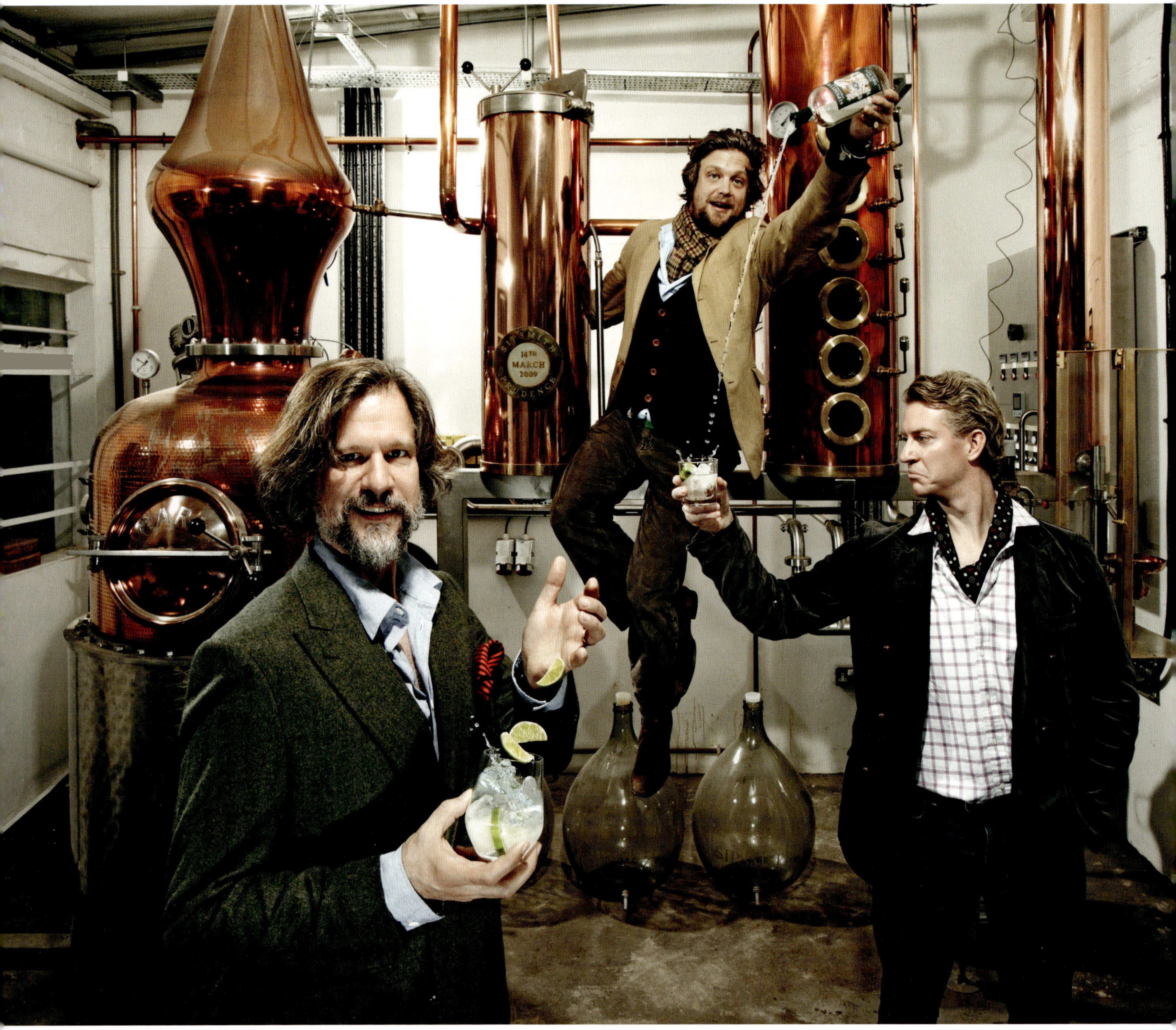
14TH
MARCH
2009

2014/15
CoolBrands.uk.com

Sipsmith

Trailblazers of London's distilling revival, Sipsmith is on a mission to bring uncompromising quality to the world of gin, handcrafting its spirits with a fetishistical love.

In 2009 the Sipsmiths – Sam, Fairfax and Jared – launched the first copper distillery in London for 189 years, bringing the lost art of traditional small batch gin distillation back to the city where it all began. From unassuming beginnings on a quiet residential street, Sipsmith is now enjoyed by discerning spirit sippers the world over. Passionately committed to its handcrafted ethos, this band of brothers is a pioneer in the golden renaissance of gin appreciation.

SIPSMITH
independent spirits

sipsmith.com

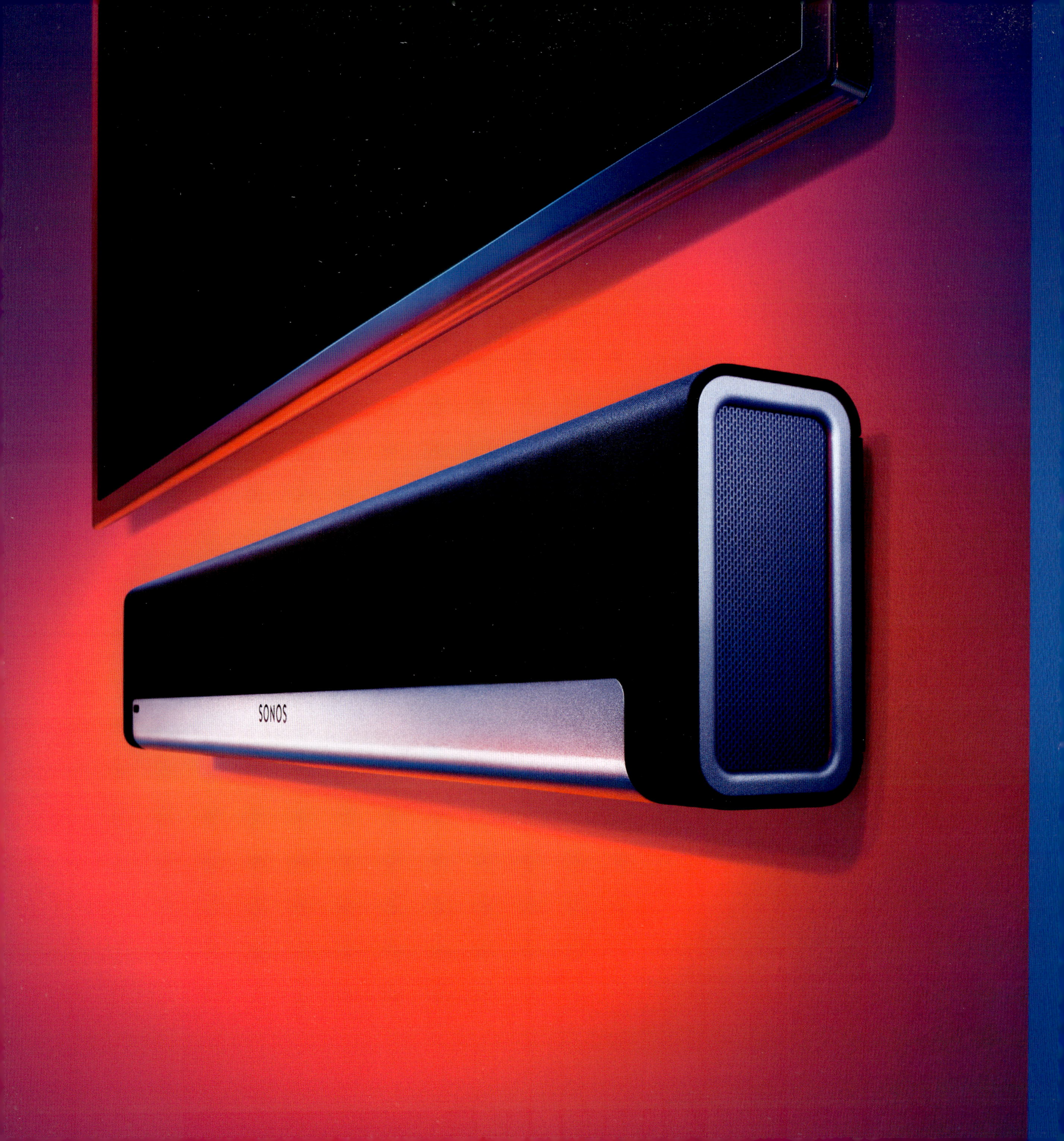
SONOS

2014/15
CoolBrands.uk.com

Sonos

In 2002 Sonos set a goal to fill every home with music. Today it continues to change the way people experience music, one home at a time.

Redefining hi-fi for the digital era, Sonos is bringing the most magical parts of music listening into the present. It is a hi-fi for anyone who wants to connect with the music they love and discover new music in a simple, engaging way. A pure and natural connection between music lovers and their music, Sonos makes complex technology feel intuitive and invisible but, most importantly, it sounds amazing. Welcome to the listening revolution.

SONOS®

sonos.com

PHARRELL WILLIAMS

HAPPY

| FROM **DESPICABLE ME 2** |

2014/15
CoolBrands.uk.com

Sony Music

Home to some of the most famous artists and labels in the world, Sony Music is constantly driven to connect artists to audiences and opportunities.

Last year, Sony drove global campaigns for artists including Beyoncé, Calvin Harris and Pharrell Williams. It developed groundbreaking partnerships like Xperia Access, an online channel that tied in the power of Sony Mobile, Vevo and The Guardian for emerging artists. It also leads a revitalised compilation market with projects including the award-winning Trevor Nelson Collection. Emerging new stars such as George Ezra, Rita Ora, Laura Mvula, Kodaline, Ella Henderson and Tom Odell joined a burgeoning UK artist roster.

sonymusic.com

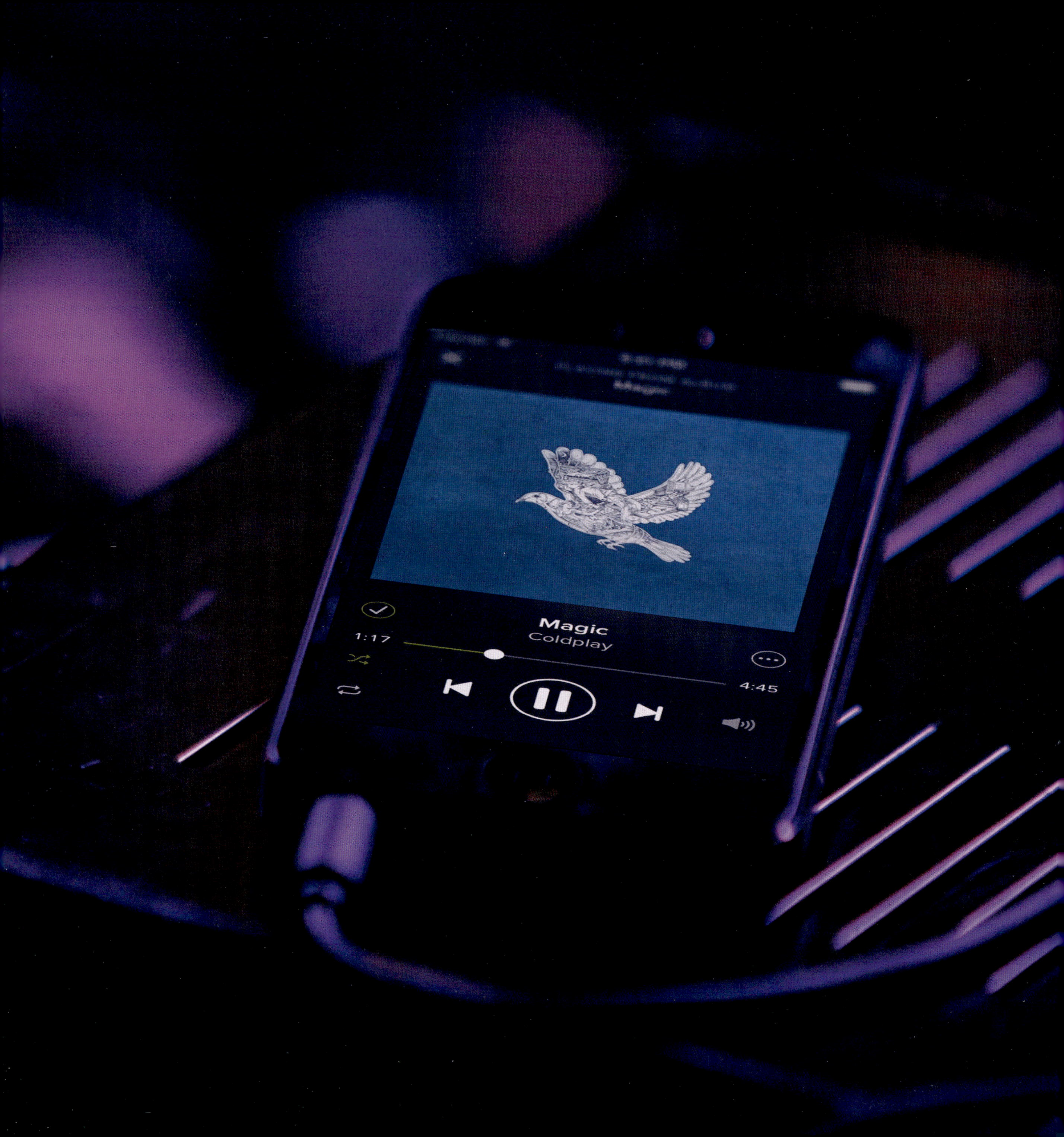
Magic
Coldplay
1:17
4:45

2014/15
CoolBrands.uk.com

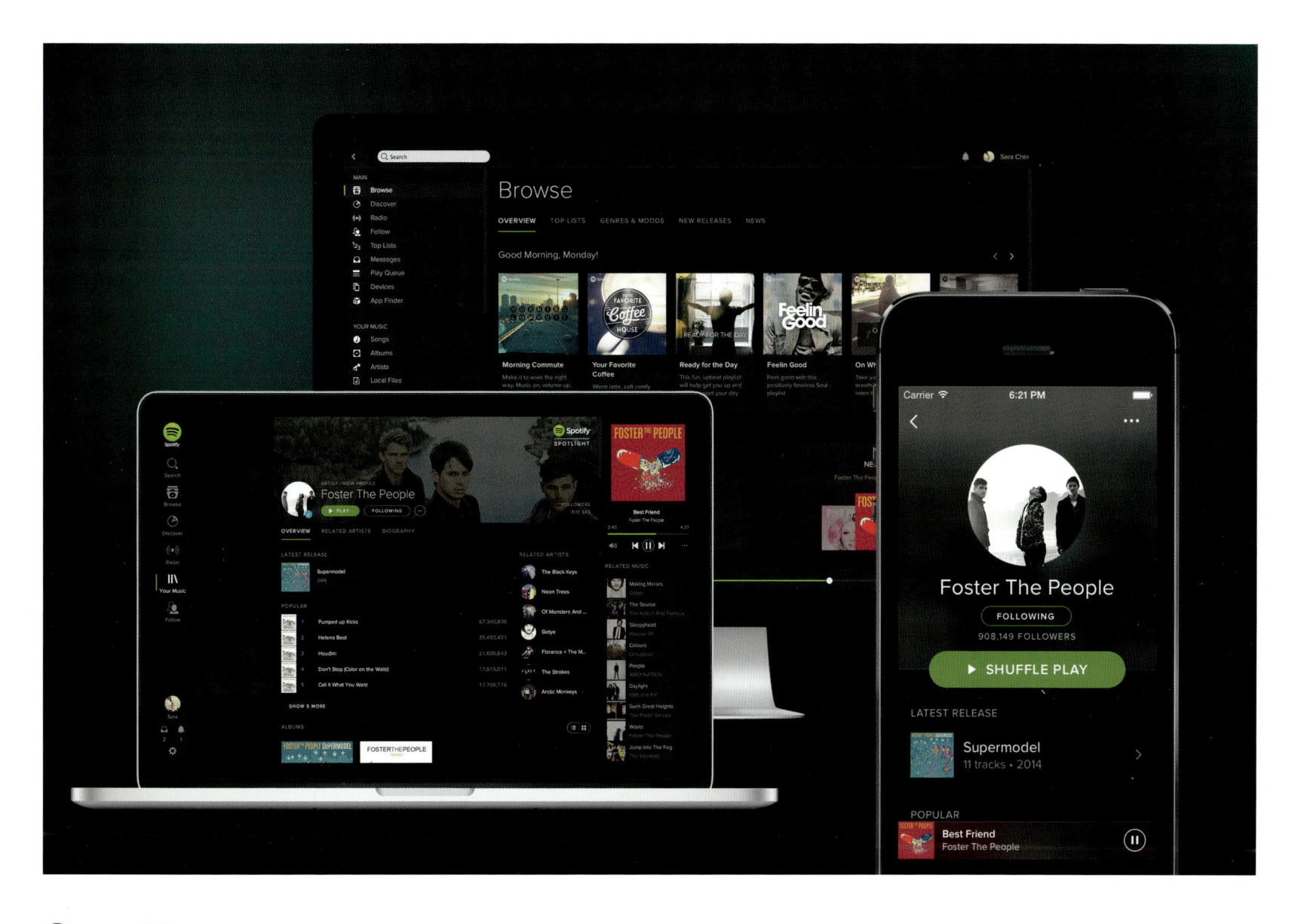

Spotify

With millions of songs available in an instant, Spotify has the right music for every moment – on computers, mobiles, tablets, home entertainment systems and more.

Spotify's dream is to make all the world's music available instantly to everyone, wherever and whenever they want it. Making it easier than ever to discover, manage and share music with friends, Spotify also makes sure that artists get a fair deal. Since launching in 2008 users have created more than 1.5 billion playlists. Now available in 57 markets globally, Spotify has more than 40 million active users and in excess of 10 million paying subscribers.

spotify.com

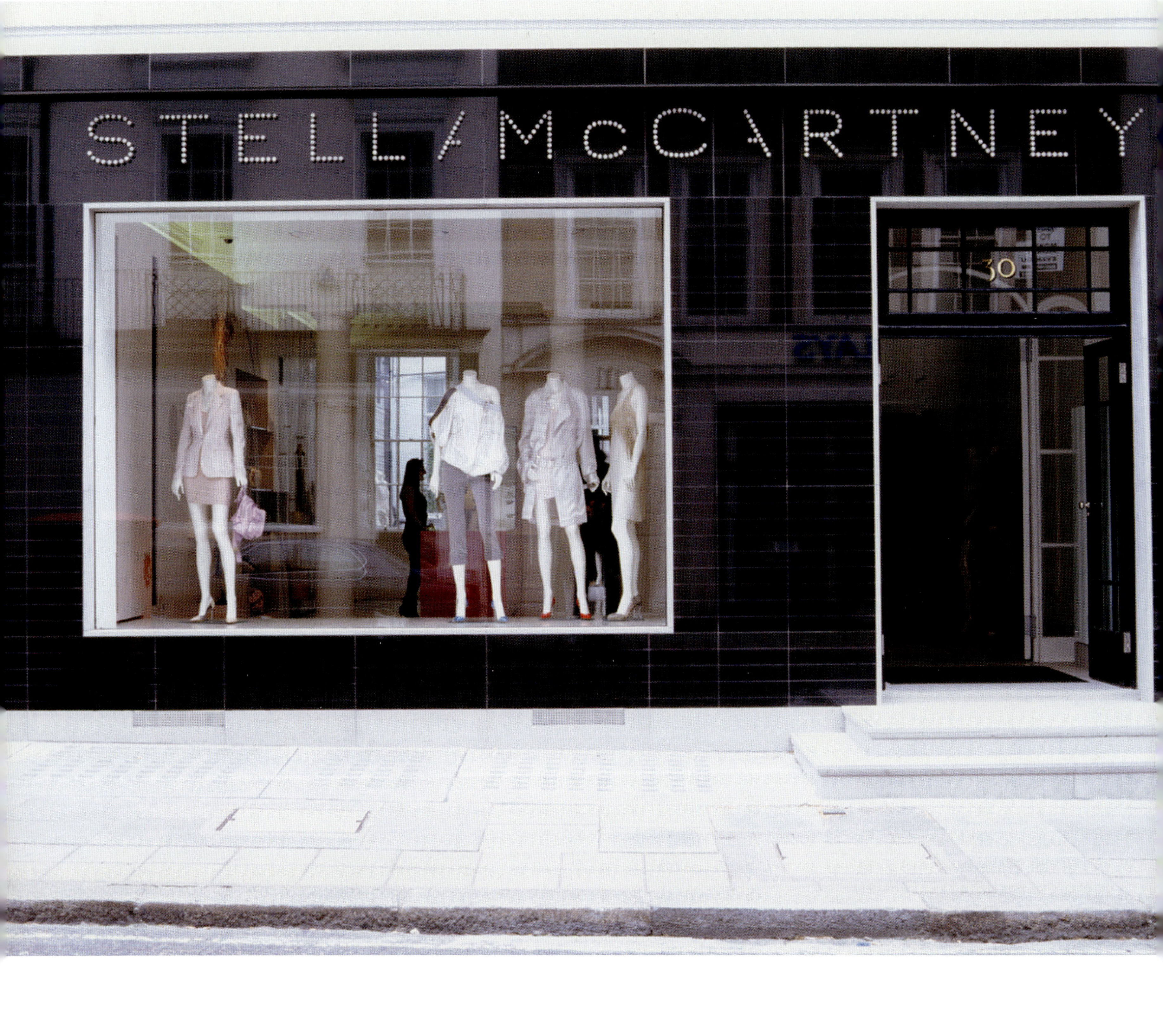
STELLA McCARTNEY
30

2014/15
CoolBrands.uk.com

Stella McCartney

A strict fur- and leather-free philosophy, coupled with her signature style of sharp tailoring and sexy femininity, has sealed Stella McCartney's place as one of Britain's most lauded designers.

Stella McCartney's eponymous ready-to-wear and accessories collection, launched in 2001, was followed by fragrances, lingerie, sunglasses and kids' collections. Now operating in 25 freestanding stores, her collections are distributed in more than 50 countries. In 2013, she received the ELLE Style Award for Best International Designer and was presented with an OBE for services to fashion. The brand has also launched its fragrance L.I.L.Y Absolute, the Stella lingerie range, eco-friendly sunglasses and an inaugural optical range.

stellamccartney.com

VOGUE

The Great BRITISH MODEL Takeover

LIFTING THE LID ON SUPERFOODS

COLOUR COMBINATION AND CU...
The new sty... equatio...

20 BRILLIA... BEAU... UPDAT...

MO... CALIFORN... LA st... sty...

2014/15
CoolBrands.uk.com

Storm

With 27 years' experience in developing the careers of fashion's most famous faces, Storm manages the brightest talents in fashion, beauty and broadcast media.

Offering expert guidance and fostering longevity in careers based on talent and integrity, Storm's clients include Cara Delevingne, Kate Moss, Jourdan Dunn and Lily Cole. Parallel to the modelling division, Special Bookings offers endorsement, image management, licensing and brand extension opportunities for models and personalities in film, music and fashion. Storm Artists manages talent including Jamie Laing, Bip Ling and Ella Catliff across broadcast media and has recently taken on YouTube influencers Essie Button, Patricia Bright and Amelia Liana.

stormmodels.com

storm
model management

Styler
Elite
Splash
Magic Flowerpot
Original
Salon Elite
Aqua Splash

2014/15
CoolBrands.uk.com

Tangle Teezer

Invented by former hair colourist Shaun P, 10 million Tangle Teezers have been sold since launching in 2007. A true innovation, the brand has achieved cult status worldwide.

Manufactured and made in the UK, Tangle Teezer is proud to be British but loved globally. A design first, and referred to as the 'life changing' hairbrush, it is now sold in over 65 countries at a rate of 10 per minute. Its unrivalled results have made it a firm favourite with professional hair stylists, beauty editors and models alike. With more revolutionary technology on the way, Tangle Teezer is set to wow the hair industry all over again.

TANGLE TEEZER®
CARES FOR THE HAIR YOU WEAR™

tangleteezer.com

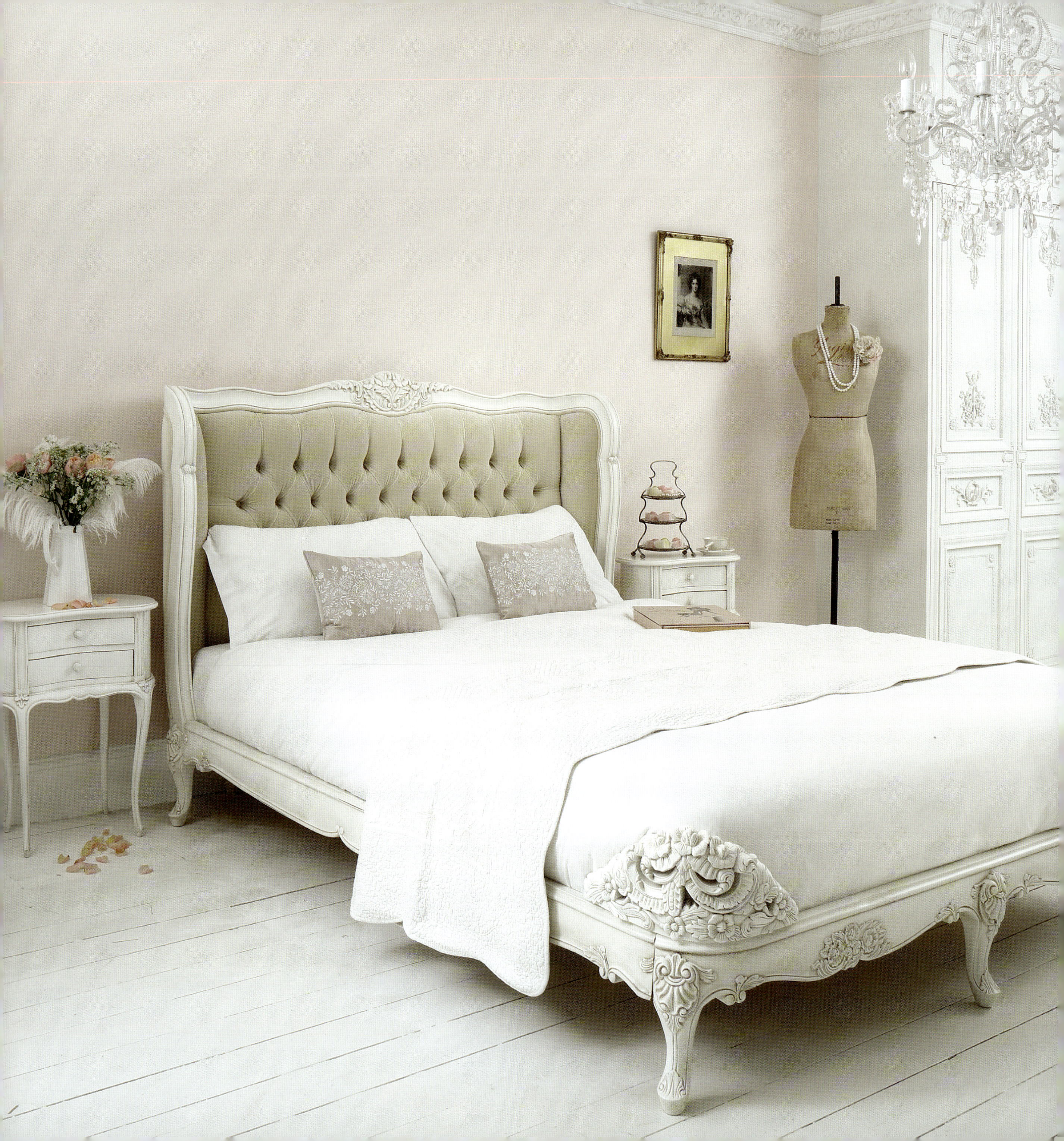

2014/15
CoolBrands.uk.com

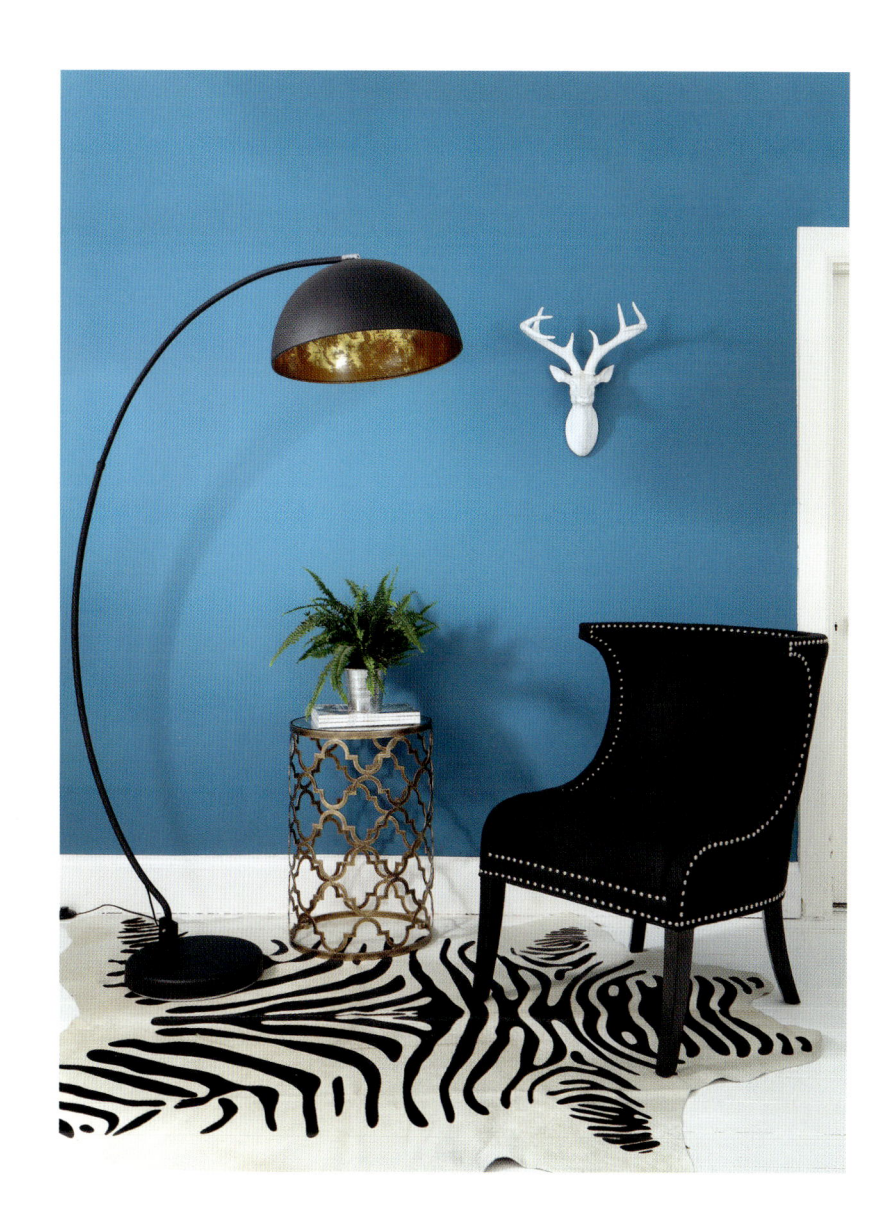

The French Bedroom Company

Combining classic French furniture with playful, progressive design, The French Bedroom Company has revolutionised bedroom styling, with super luxe interiors and accessories that ooze high-octane glamour.

The French Bedroom Company was born in May 2006 with a simple ethos: to offer French furniture that exudes elegance and injects overstated beauty and sassy, playful style into interiors. It combines enchanting Louis XV-style furniture with a touch of the unexpected in its contemporary lighting and accessories. Effortless luxe meets edgy minimalism – this is interior design that makes a statement, starts a conversation and transforms the mundane into the magnificent.

THE
French
Bedroom
COMPANY

frenchbedroomcompany.co.uk

Mills & Boon
TRUE LOVE
Stories
Mills & Boon
The
HONEYMOON
is OVER!
TRUE LOVE STORIES

2014/15
CoolBrands.uk.com

Interiors by Mike Tinney | Portraits by Tom Oldham Photography

The House of St Barnabas

Supporting London's homeless back into sustained work, The House of St Barnabas integrates an Employment Academy into its not-for-profit private members' club in Soho.

Supporting London's homeless back into work through its not-for-profit members' club, The House of St Barnabas offers integrated on-site training and work experience. The charity has been named one of the Deloitte Social Innovation Pioneers and shortlisted by Social Enterprise UK's 'Ones to Watch'. Described as a 'hip Soho hang-out' by the Financial Times' How to Spend It, the culturally inspired club is also succeeding in 'demolishing stereotypes' according to Dazed Digital.

The House of St Barnabas
LONDON

hosb.org.uk

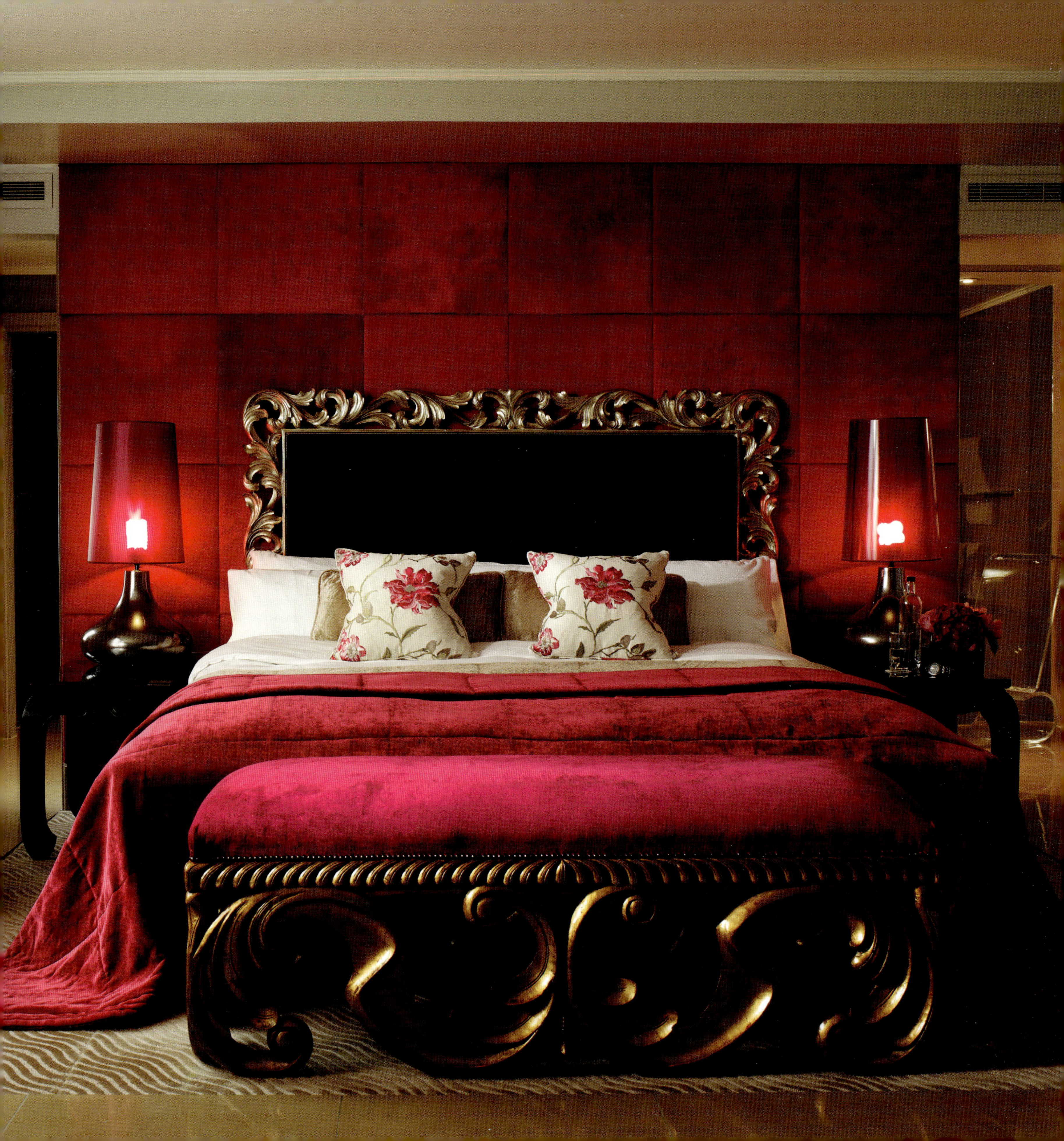

2014/15
CoolBrands.uk.com

The May Fair

There are luxury hotels and then there is The May Fair: an icon of expressive contemporary design, bringing together boutique attention to detail with impeccable service.

With a glamorous heritage dating back to 1927, The May Fair offers more than 400 luxury bedrooms, nestled right in the heart of London. Guests can unwind in the spa, feast at the hotel's destination restaurant, the May Fair Kitchen, delight in a film screening or performance relayed live from the London Stage in the private cinema, or try their luck in the casino. Alive with the energy of its central location, remarkable experiences await behind every door.

THE MAY FAIR

themayfairhotel.co.uk

The O2

2014/15
CoolBrands.uk.com

The O2

As the world's most popular music and entertainment venue, The O2 consistently excites, thrills and wows millions of fans with unforgettable experiences.

Since 2007, the unique hands-on collaboration between O2 and AEG has seen The O2 become the multi-award winning home of world-class entertainment. The 20,000 capacity arena has hosted Prince, Monty Python, the BRITs, ATP tennis, Led Zeppelin and more. But that's not all. With attractions like Up at The O2, Brooklyn Bowl, Cineworld as well as 24 bars and restaurants, The O2 offers a huge range of experiences all under one iconic roof.

theo2.co.uk

THE SAUCY FISH CO.

NO TOUCH NO SMELL NO FUSS

FOIL BAKE BAG

VINTAGE CHEDDAR & CHIVE SAUCE

SMASHING WITH SMOKED HADDOCK

240g ℮
SERVES 1-2

Serving suggestion

2014/15
CoolBrands.uk.com

The Saucy Fish Co.

The ultimate inspiration for food lovers, The Saucy Fish Co. pairs fish fillets with tasty sauces for fish dishes, minus the fuss.

On a mission to put more fish on dinner tables, The Saucy Fish Co. has transformed the way millions of Brits think about fish. With recent launches in the US and Australia, the young brand is set to emulate this success overseas. Uncovering the fact that cooking fish can feel a bit daunting, The Saucy Fish Co. launched a range that cuts out the fuss and hard work. Hey Presto! A shoal of inspiring fish and sauce combinations.

thesaucyfishco.com

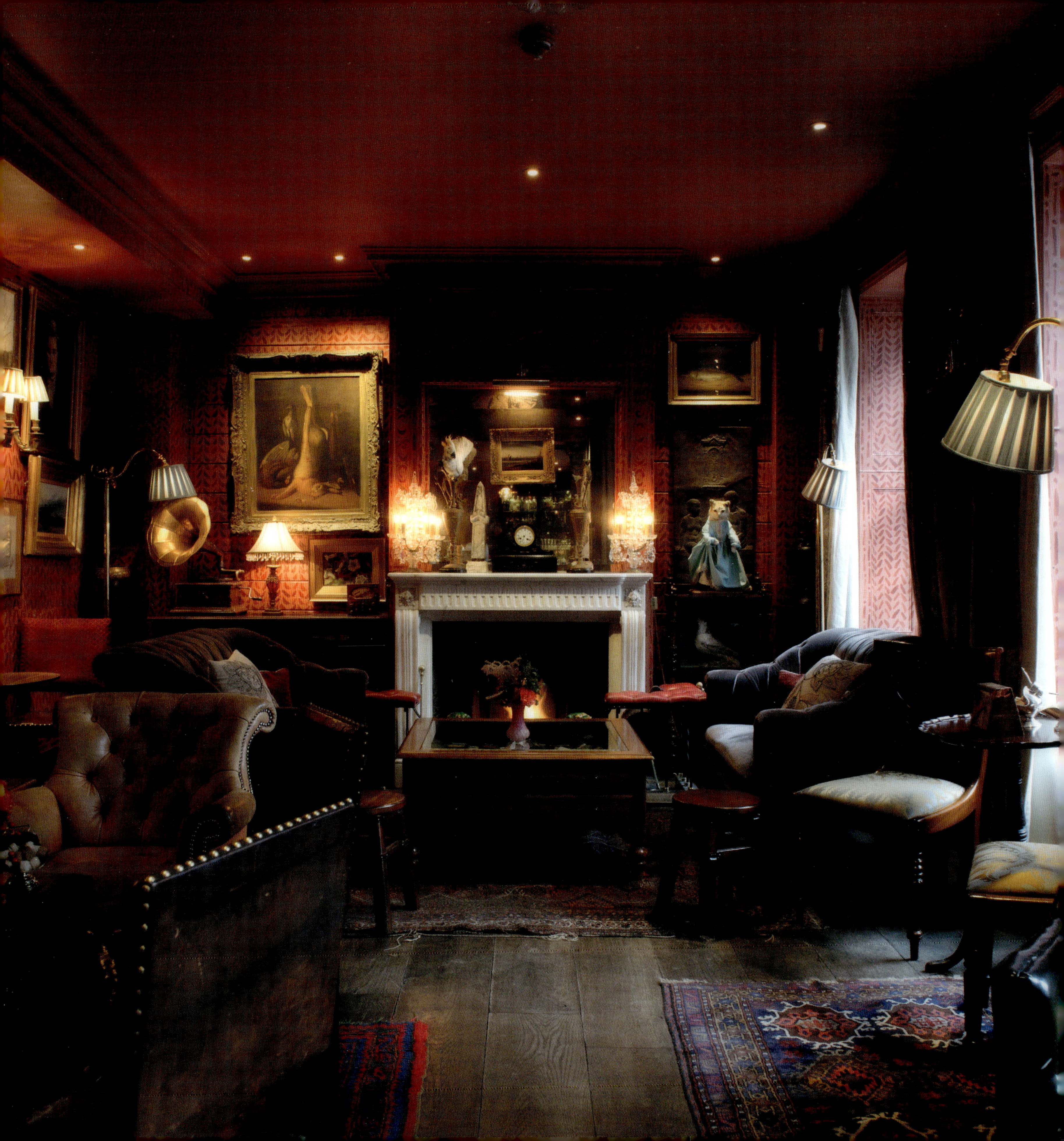

2014/15
CoolBrands.uk.com

The Zetter Townhouse

Like the private home of an eccentric ancestor, The Zetter Townhouse is a magical, Alice in Wonderland meets Charles Dickens experience that delights at every turn.

Created by the Zetter Group, this 13-bedroom Georgian townhouse and cocktail lounge has reinterpreted the boutique hotel concept. Overlooking a charming cobbled square, the townhouse features a sumptuous lounge stuffed full of curiosities, where an apothecary bar dispenses exceptional cocktails. Meanwhile, bedrooms – from the whimsical to the majestic – offer a luxurious antidote to any revelry enjoyed in the lounge below. A new addition to the family – The Zetter Townhouse, Marylebone – is due to open in October 2014.

thezettertownhouse.com

The Zetter Townhouse

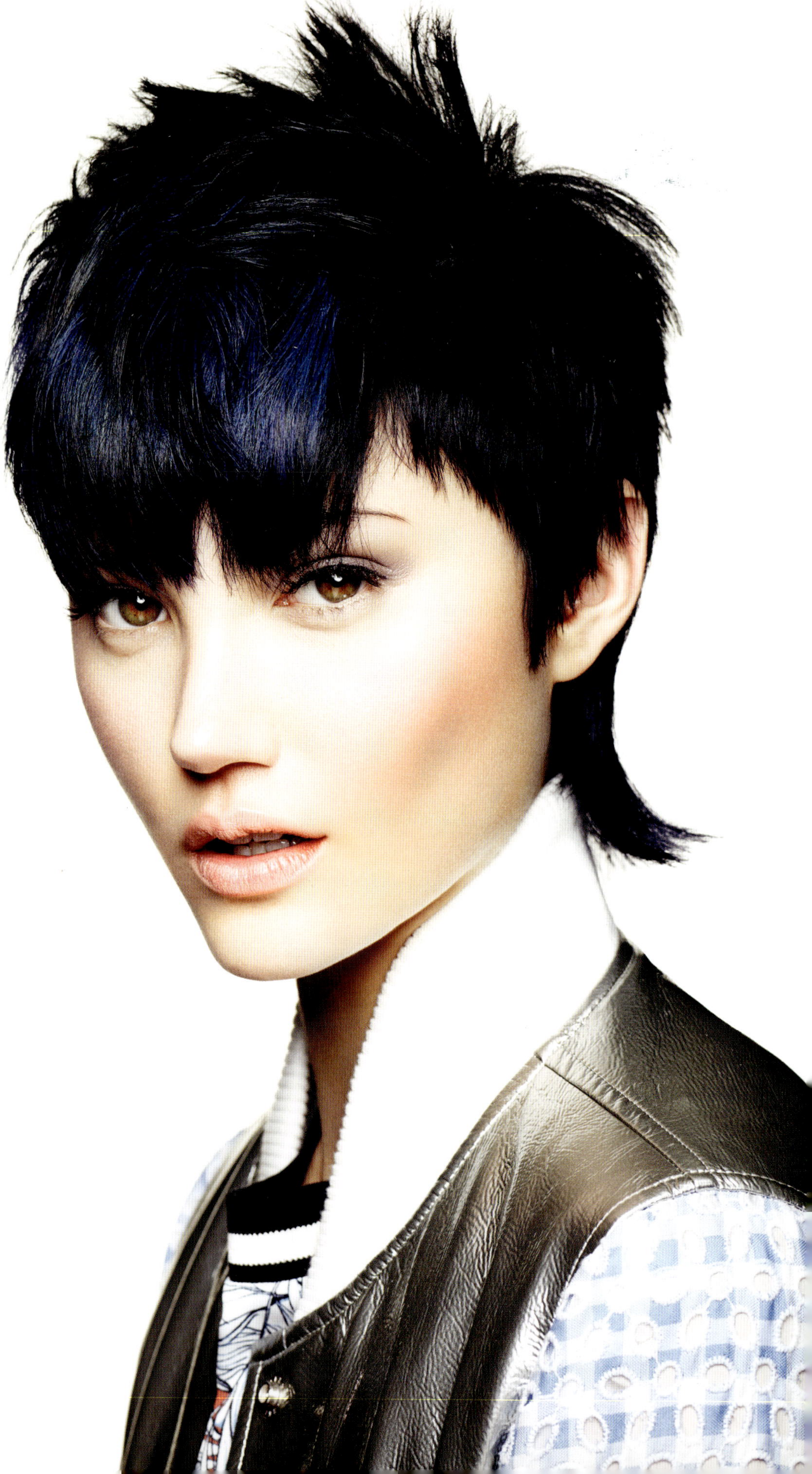

2014/15
CoolBrands.uk.com

TONI&GUY

Having celebrated 50 years of hair, fashion and heritage in 2013, TONI&GUY is a renowned innovator within the hair industry, bridging the gap between high fashion and hairdressing.

One of the most powerful hairdressing brands in the world, with more than 400 salons in 50 countries, TONI&GUY has helped to change the face of the hairdressing industry on an international scale. Providing the ultimate link between fashion and hair, 2014 marks its 10th year as Official Sponsor of London Fashion Week. Furthermore, its professional haircare range, label.m, will celebrate 10 years as the Official Product of London Fashion Week in 2015.

toniandguy.com

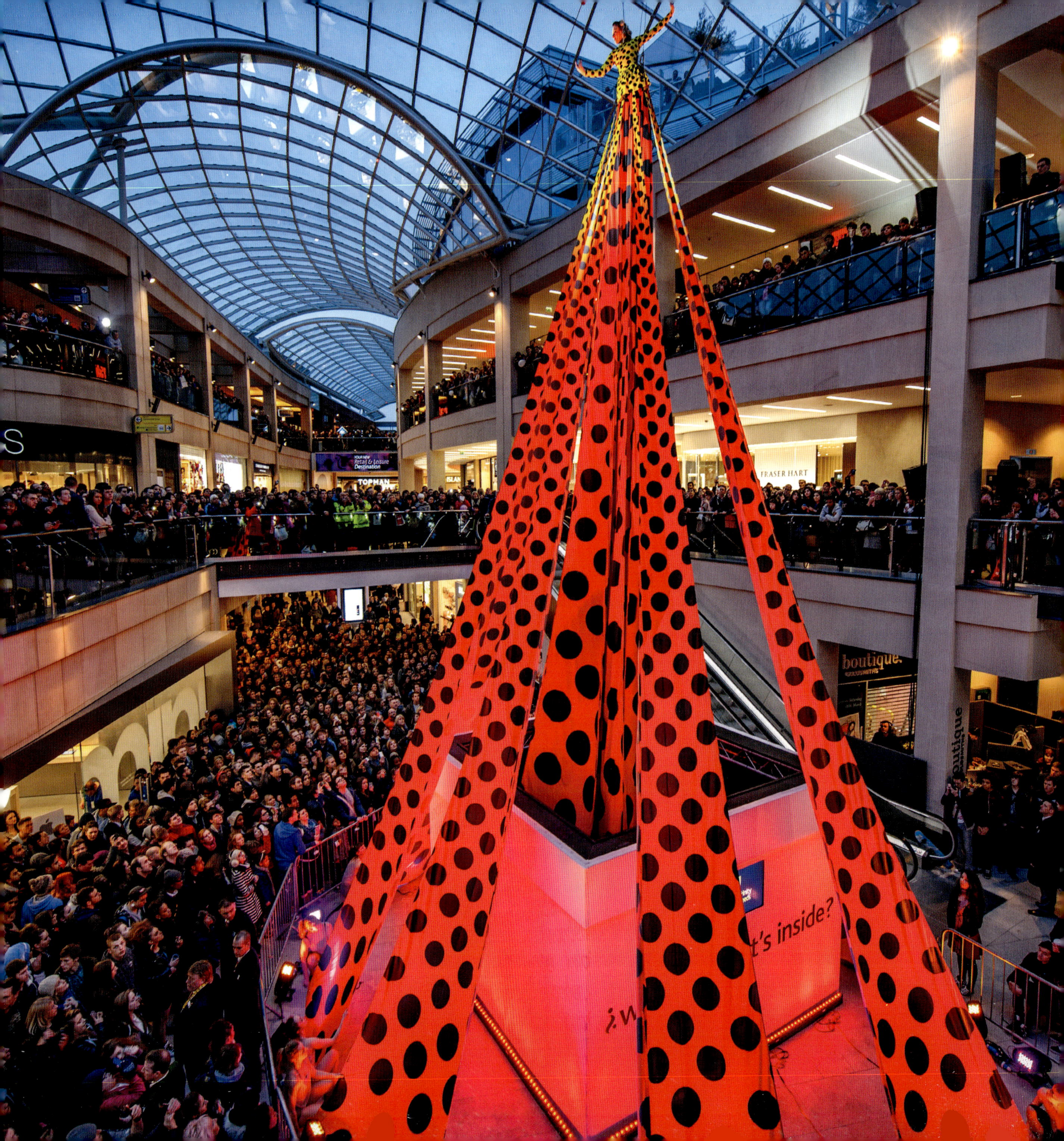
TOPMAN
FRASER HART
boutique
t's inside?

2014/15
CoolBrands.uk.com

Trinity Leeds

An exceptional mix of fashion, food and film, together with its pioneering digital experience, makes Trinity Leeds a mall unlike any other.

Designed for the city's fashion conscious, mobile savvy and technologically advanced, Trinity Leeds redefines experiential shopping and dining. Beneath a dramatic sweeping glazed roof, four levels of open arcades house 110 shops and restaurants. The one million sq ft city centre destination has brought 65 new national and international brands to Leeds for the first time, and hosts a groundbreaking mix of authentic street food, rooftop fine dining, cocktail bars and balcony restaurants.

trinityleeds.com

tunetribe ENTERTAINMENT STORE

JUST A CLICK AWAY

2014/15
CoolBrands.uk.com

tunetribe
ENTERTAINMENT STORE

MP3	eBooks	CDs	Books	DVDs
Tickets	Vinyl	Podcasts	Audio Books	Artist Services

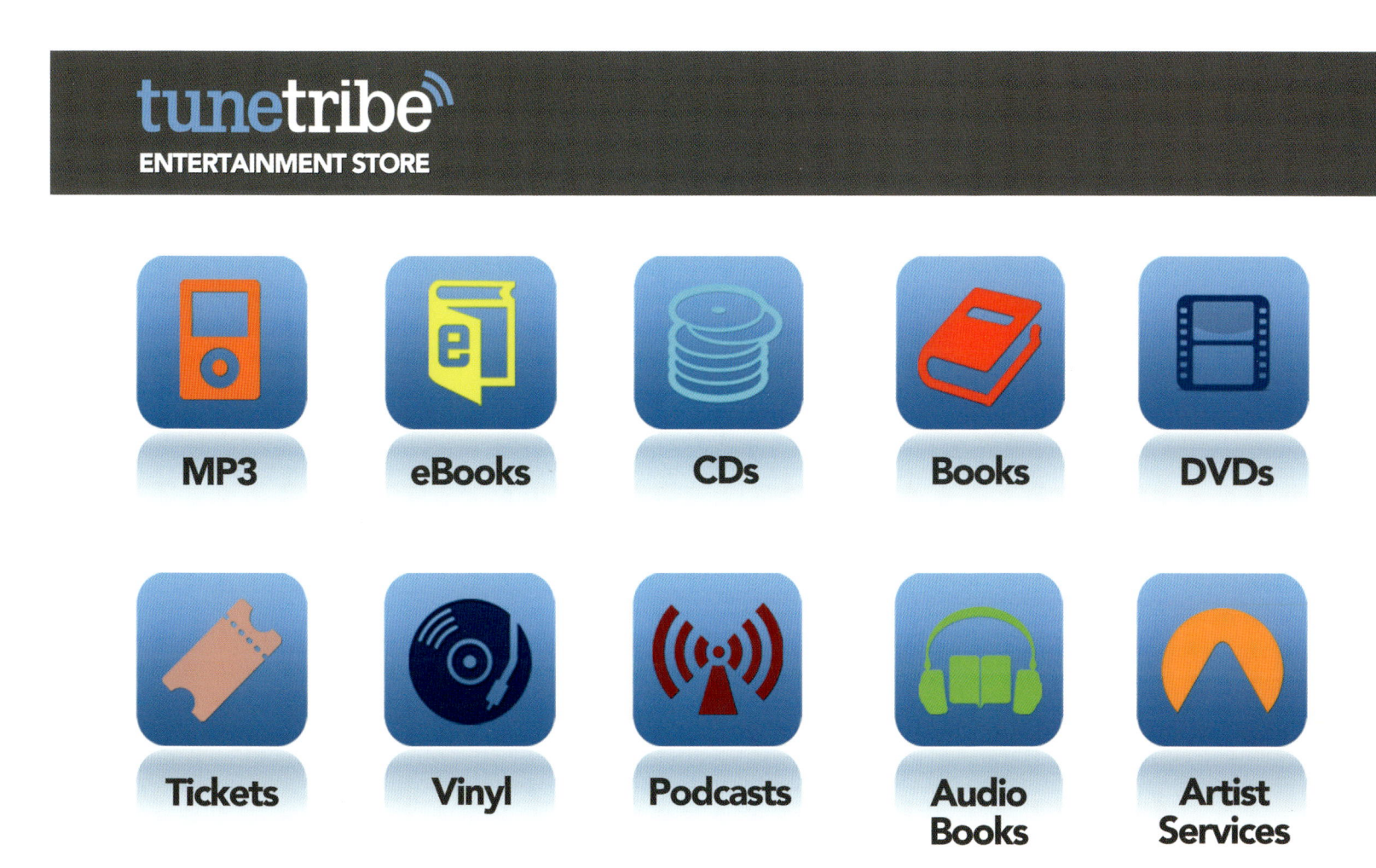

Tunetribe

Now much more than a music store, Tunetribe has evolved over the past year and added exciting new products for everyone's entertainment needs.

With a new landing page and an exciting new look to its product pages with enhanced functionality, Tunetribe is the ultimate digital entertainment store. In addition, through Tunetribe Digital, brands are able to utilise its industry expertise in music, books and digital development to create exciting programmes and affiliate deals. It provides a variety of services such as e-vouchers for all of its products and white label sites if required. All just a click away.

tunetribe

tunetribe.com

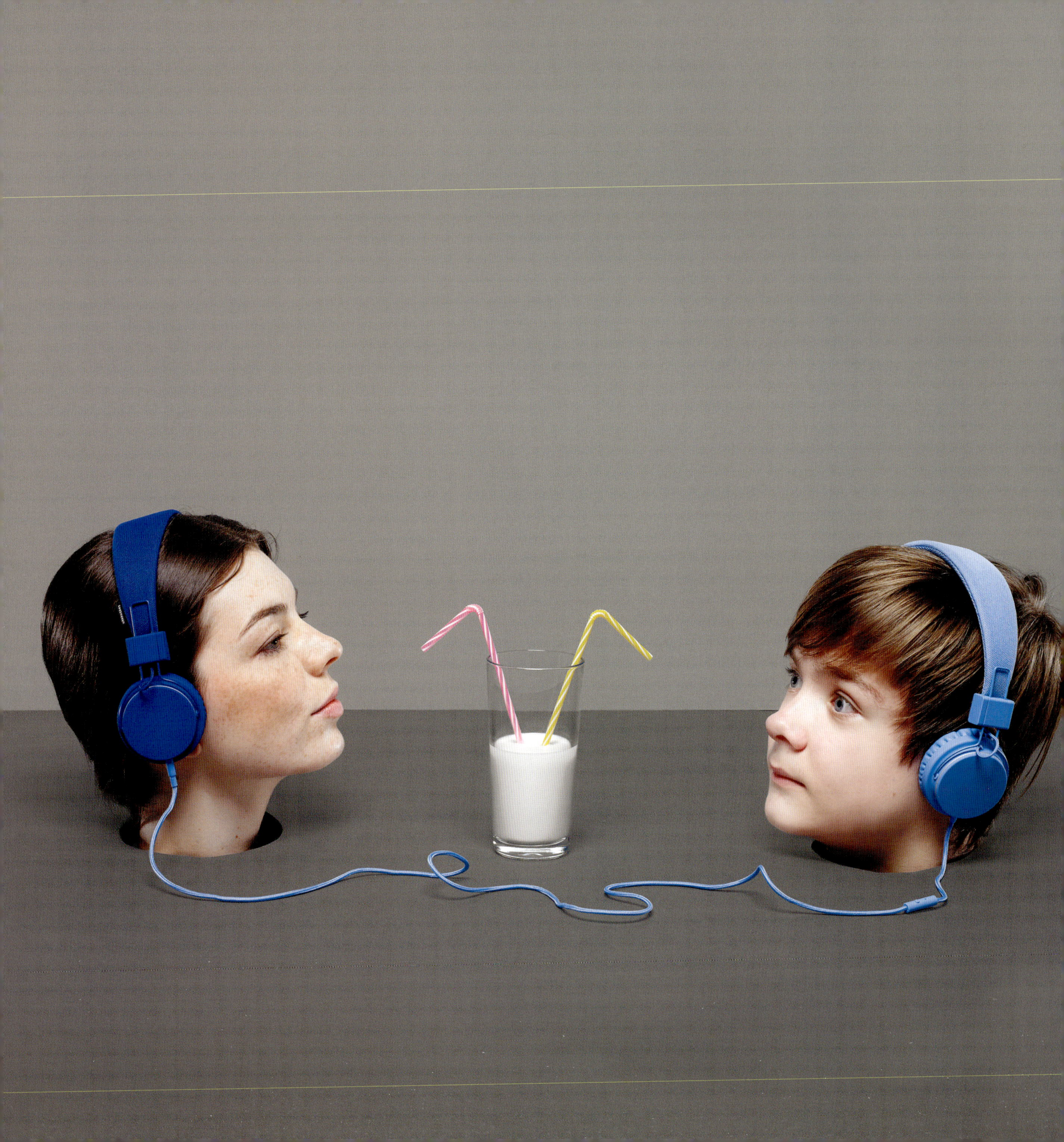

2014/15
CoolBrands.uk.com

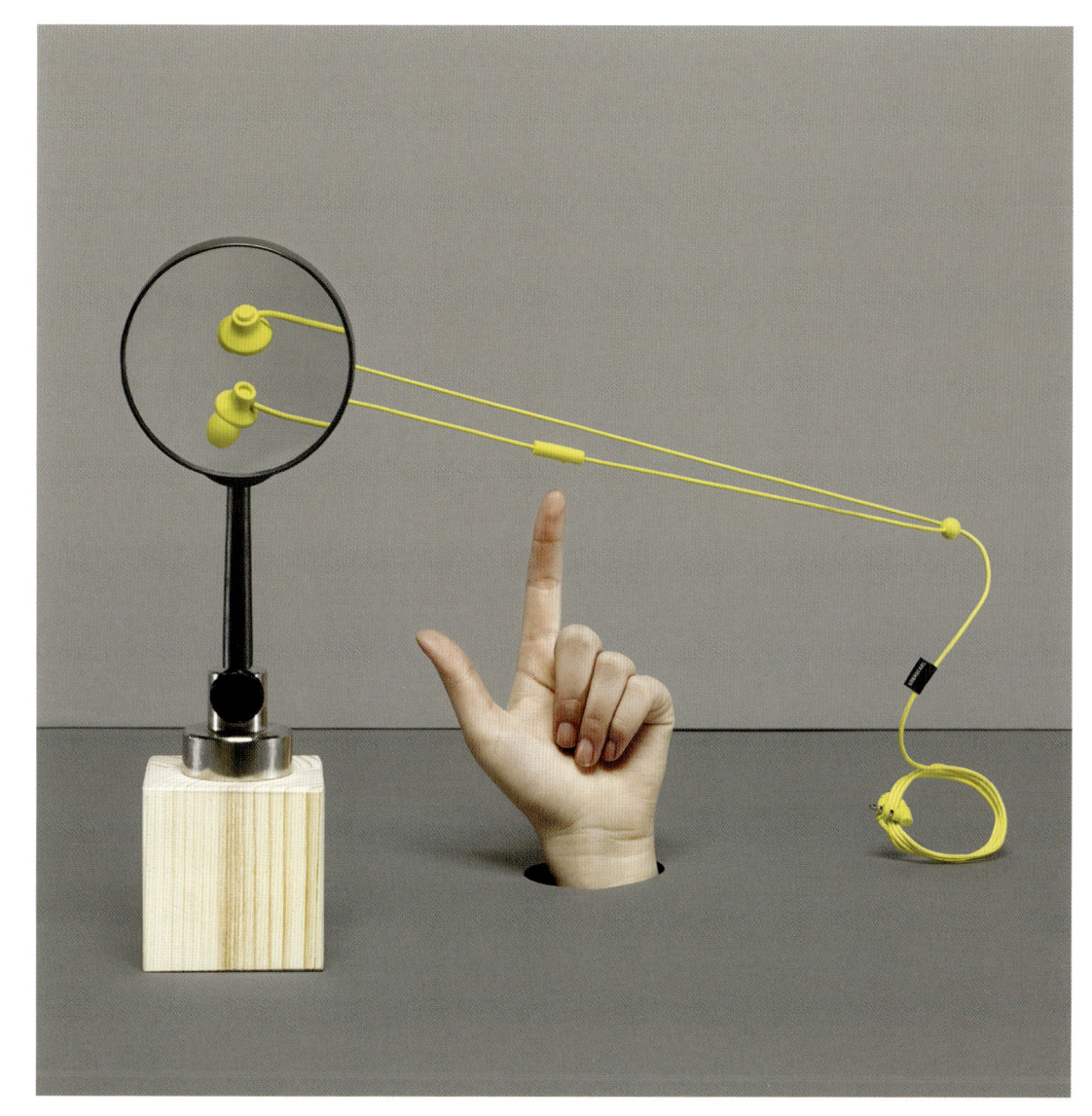

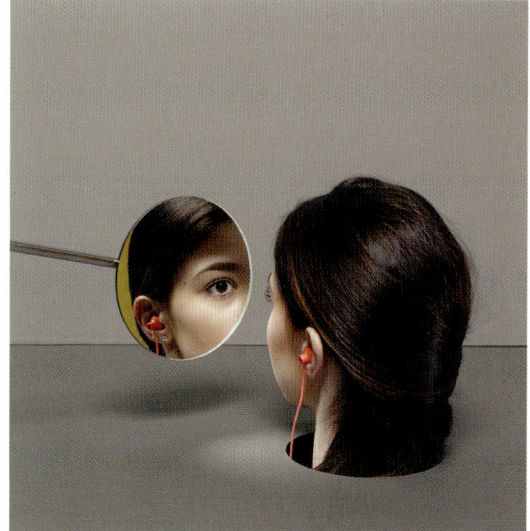

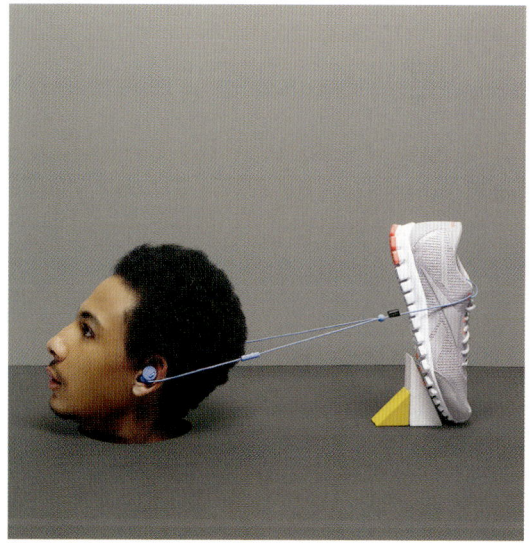

Urbanears

Making headphones that fit everyday life, Urbanears supplies the perfect listening device for anyone with a pocket full of music and a wish to make the most of it.

Urbanears has built its success upon a few simple ingredients – great design, innovative features and lots and lots of colour. These building blocks are what has helped catapult Urbanears into 90 countries (and growing) worldwide, and changed the perception of how people think of headphones. Other companies may try to emulate the brand, but Urbanears is the original in colourful headphones.

URBANEARS™

urbanears.com

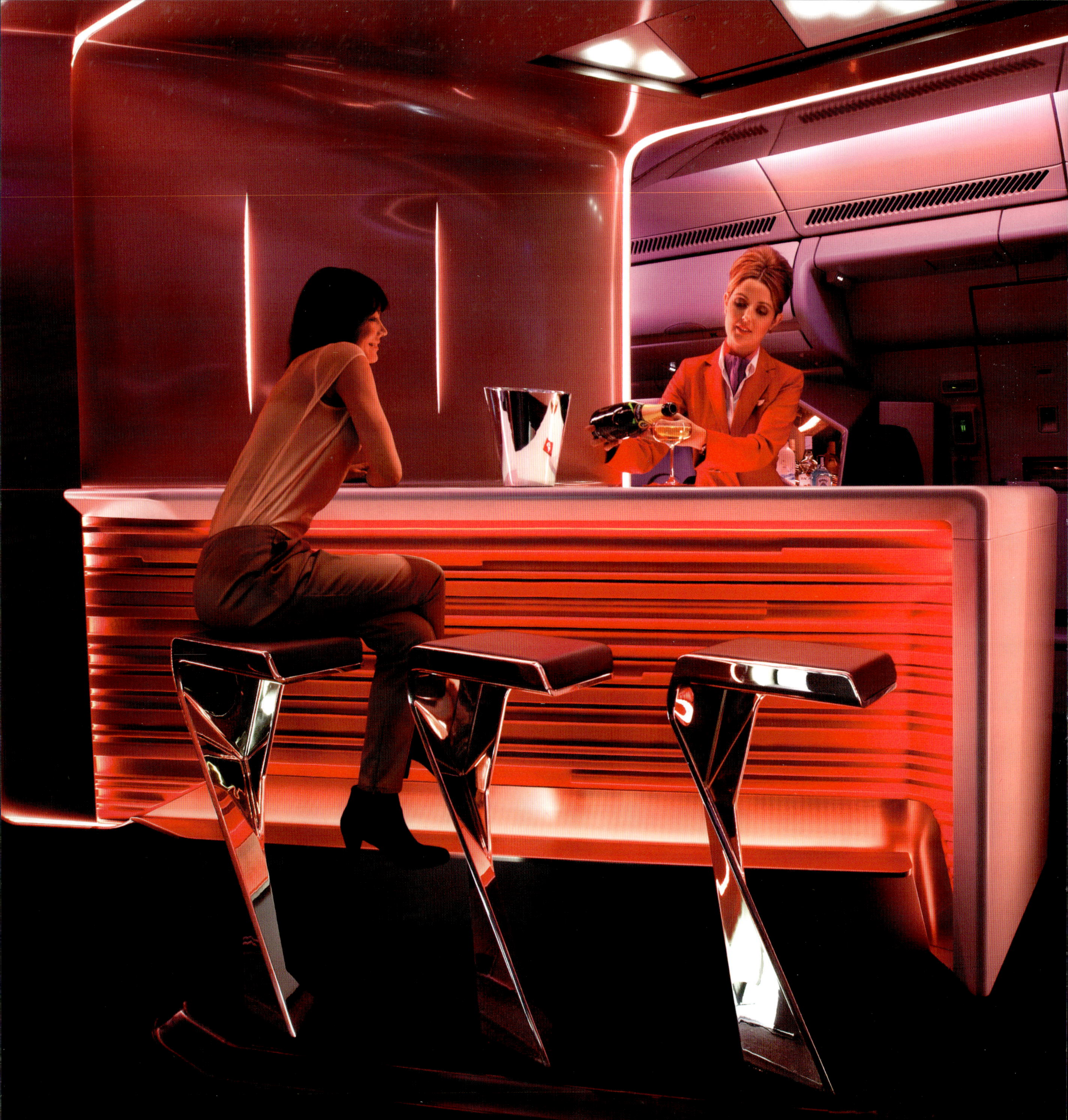

2014/15
CoolBrands.uk.com

Virgin Atlantic

Exciting innovations, famously friendly service and a unique spirit make Virgin Atlantic a true brand of choice. It's an airline that just loves to fly.

Virgin Atlantic flies six million people a year to more than 30 of the world's most popular destinations. From luxurious Upper Class bars and Clubhouse lounges to an award-winning inflight entertainment system, it offers a taste of the glamour of travel, lost to so many airlines today. Now in its 30th birthday year, a new Vivienne Westwood designed uniform is helping its people deliver, with renewed style and confidence, the unique service that customers love.

virgin atlantic

virgin-atlantic.com

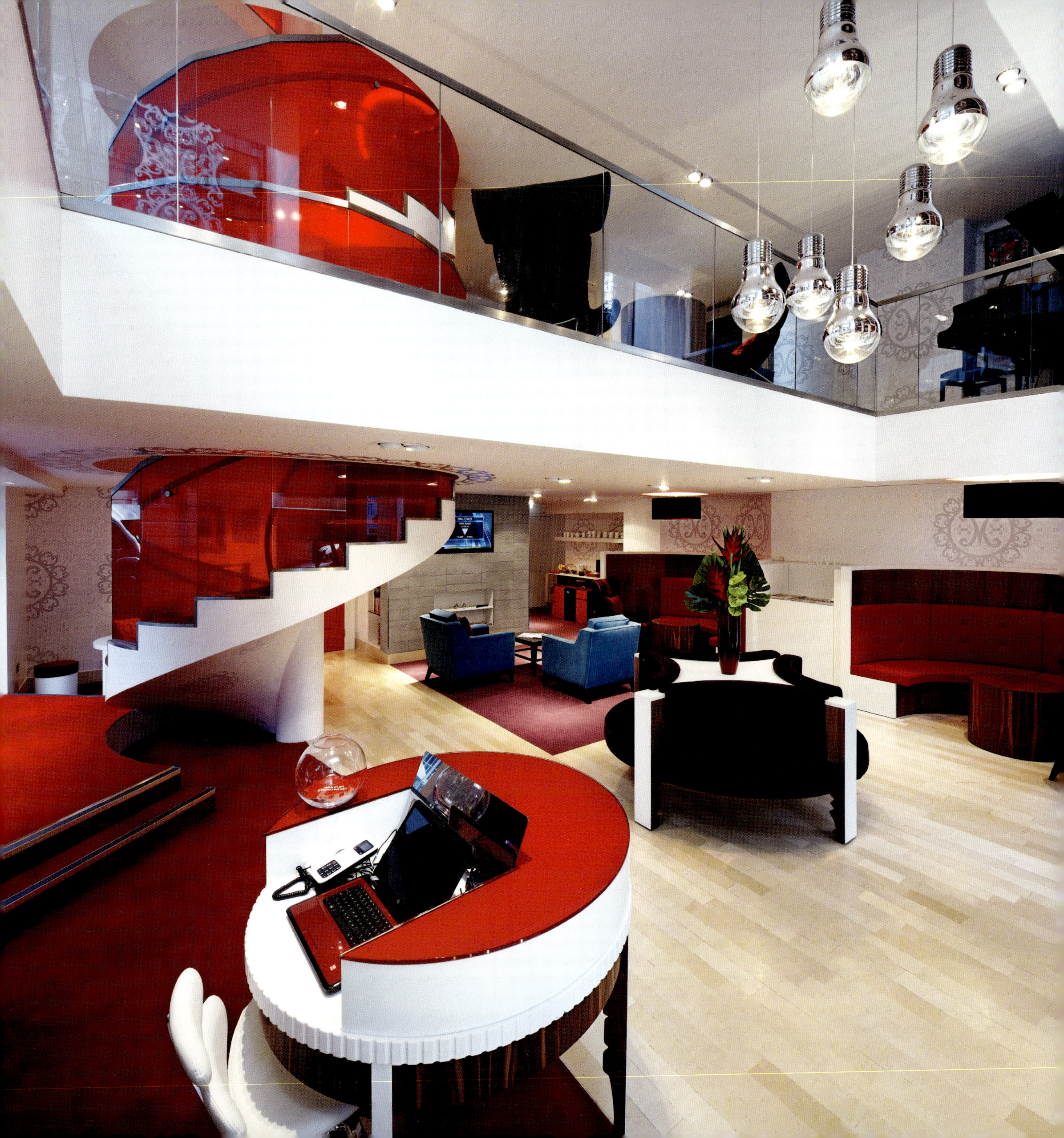

2014/15
CoolBrands.uk.com

Virgin Money

The Virgin brand has been shaking up various industries for more than 40 years. Now Virgin Money is on a quest to make banking better.

Building on its reputation for simple and straightforward products, Virgin Money has moved onto the high street, challenging the conventions of how a bank should behave. Gone are boring branches, replaced by warm and inviting Stores and exclusive customer Lounges. And its not-for-profit fundraising website, Virgin Money Giving, shows a brand keen to use its expertise with money to do some good in the world. For those who'd like their bank to be a little less banky.

virginmoney.com

Expert Council
2014/15

Much more than merely a 'trend', coolness is a distinctive, elusive quality. It can be found in many things, but can never be forced. So how do we decide who makes the CoolBrands® cut? Our Expert Council – a hand-picked team of 37 style gurus, fashion leaders, instigators and innovators – were tasked with separating the coolest from all the rest.

Chairman, CoolBrands® Expert Council

Stephen Cheliotis
Chief Executive, The Centre for Brand Analysis (TCBA)
@TCBA_London

A leading brand commentator and consultant, Stephen's work at TCBA includes brand evaluation and perception studies, strategic planning for brand owners and market analysis. Stephen also produces studies for agencies, speaks at conferences, comments on branding issues for the media and acts as an expert witness in brand disputes.

Bip Ling
Blogger, DJ & Model
@BipLing

A major influence in the world of social media, Bip is also a DJ, artist and one of the fashion industry's foremost bloggers at bipling.com. Having fronted numerous high end campaigns for Louis Vuitton, Nike, CK ONE Color Cosmetics and Uggs, her creativity has also led to a design collaboration with luxury shoe company Pretty Ballerinas.

Carl Barât
Musician & Actor
@carlbaratmusic

Charli XCX
Singer
@charli_xcx

Charlotte Riley
Actress

Former frontman of The Libertines and Dirty Pretty Things, Carl's eponymous debut solo album was released in 2010. Following numerous theatrical appearances, including Pop'pea at Théâtre du Châtelet in Paris, Carl dueted with Vanessa Paradis on her forthcoming album. Now focusing on songwriting, Carl is working in the studio with Johnny Marr, Andy Burrows and Ed Harcourt.

A 22 year-old pop sensation, Charli XCX released two free mixtapes through SoundCloud before her EP, You're The One, launched in June 2012. Following a tour with Santigold and Coldplay the same year, Charli's debut album, True Romance, was released in April 2013 to rave reviews. Following the release of her single SuperLove, Charli is working on a follow-up album.

After playing Sarah Hurst in Easy Virtue, Charlotte went on to star as Catherine Earnshaw in ITV's adaptation of Wuthering Heights. Recent projects include the film Heart of the Sea, and starring alongside Tom Cruise in Edge of Tomorrow. Charlotte has also joined the cast of BBC's Peaky Blinders and Jonathan Strange & Mr Norrell.

2014/15
CoolBrands.uk.com

David Harewood MBE
Actor
@DavidHarewood

Eleanor Tomlinson
Actress

Ella Eyre
Singer-Songwriter
@EllaEyre

A RADA graduate, David has received huge critical acclaim for his work in theatre, cinema and television. He played Captain Poison in the Oscar-nominated film Blood Diamond, starred alongside Claire Danes in hit US drama Homeland, and recently worked with Liam Neeson in the film Third Person. In 2012, David received an MBE for services to drama.

Following her first film role in The Illusionist at the age of 13, Eleanor has appeared in Angus, Thongs and Perfect Snogging, Tim Burton's Alice in Wonderland and Jack the Giant Slayer. She was seen in the White Queen and Death Comes to Pemberley on BBC One, and will soon appear in adaptations of Winston Graham's Poldark novels for the BBC.

Fierce and fearless at just 19, with a number one feature on Rudimental's Waiting All Night to her name, Ella's new breed of soul is here. Already tipped as the artist to watch by the BBC's Sound of 2014 and a BRITS Critics' Choice, the voice of 2014 is sure to have a spectacular year.

'To me, cool is being inspired by something that takes you quite by surprise. Serendipity.' **Eleanor Tomlinson**

Emily Hartridge
International YouTuber & Presenter
@emilyhartridge

Emily Johnston
Blogger
@fashionfoiegras

Gisèle Scanlon
Writer, Broadcaster, Artist & Co-Founder, thegoddessguide.com
@GoddessGuide

Rising to fame with her YouTube show 10 Reasons Why, Emily is now an internet sensation. The hugely popular show gained a following of over 140,000 subscribers, with over 1.5 million unique hits a month. She has since interviewed Hollywood A-listers such as Russell Brand, Hugh Jackman, Amanda Seyfried and Eddie Redmayne.

Founder and Editor of the hugely influential fashion news and luxury lifestyle website Fashion Foie Gras, Emily has also contributed to various other publications, including Cosmopolitan, The Huffington Post and Glamour Magazine. She has also worked with a number of prestigious brands including Ralph Lauren, Hermes, Michael Kors, Mercedes-Benz, Tommy Hilfiger and Victoria's Secret.

After more than one million people read her illustrated fashion and culture books, and now her daily blog, thegoddessguide.com, Gisèle became a publishing sensation. Her intelligent approach to culture, travel, art and fashion has won her numerous accolades, including two digital Lovie Awards from The International Academy of Digital Arts and Sciences.

'Cool isn't necessarily about luxury or exclusivity – it's about what makes a brand compelling in a world of brand-information overload.' **Tom Findlay**

2014/15
CoolBrands.uk.com

Izzy Lawrence
DJ, TV Presenter & Blogger
@Izzy_Lawrence

Jamal Edwards
Digital Entrepreneur & Founder, SB.TV
@jamaledwards

James-lee Duffy
Art Director & Illustrator, We Are Shadows
@jamesleeduffy

Izzy has DJ'd at global events including Coachella for Guess, Vogue Fashion Nights Out & The Grand Prix. As a presenter she has worked with the BBC, Sky, MTV and Sundance channel. Her blog, izzyfied.com, has recently partnered with Dazed & Confused and she writes a column on tech for The Good Web Guide.

Described as 'The Cowell of the Urban Scene', Jamal founded SB.TV aged 15, and is still CEO today. With over 200 million YouTube views, SB.TV has featured interviews with a range of guests, from Richard Branson to Bruno Mars. Jamal's business book, Self Belief: The Vision, published in 2013 and was a number one bestseller in its first week.

James has worked on brands such as Nike, Smirnoff and Nintendo. His illustration work has shown internationally and he has been commissioned by the likes of Panasonic, Dr Martens and Diesel. His zine, Pavement Licker, is found in cities across the world and has featured contributions from such names as Shepard Fairey and Banksy.

Jodie Kidd
International Model
@RealJodieKidd

Jonathan Bailey
Actor
@JonnyBailey

Julien Macdonald OBE
Fashion Designer
@JulienMacdonald

A leading supermodel, Jodie is a unique fusion of the worlds of designer fashion and glamorous sports. In addition to her hugely successful modelling career, Jodie doubles up as a Maserati racing driver. A familiar face on TV, she has appeared on Jack Osborne's Adrenalin Junkie, Strictly Come Dancing and Britain's Next Top Model.

Known for his role in the drama Broadchurch, Jonathan's other TV credits include W1A, Leonardo and Campus. He was nominated for Outstanding Newcomer at the 2012 Evening Standard Awards and recently played Cassio in Othello at the National Theatre. Film credits include Testament of Youth and What We Did on Our Holiday.

Previously Head Designer of Knitwear for CHANEL and Creative Director of Givenchy, Julien launched Julien Macdonald Bespoke – an in-house atelier dedicated to creating one-off styles, handmade in Britain – in 2012. A luminary of the fashion industry, he has dressed numerous international stars including Beyoncé, Kristen Stewart, Madonna, Rihanna, Katy Perry and Naomi Campbell.

2014/15
CoolBrands.uk.com

Justin Wilkes
DJ, Kisstory/Kiss FM UK
@justinwilkes

One of the UK's most respected music radio presenters, Justin hosts Kisstory each weekday afternoon. Also a renowned club DJ, he is famed for his sets at major product launches and for voicing advertising campaigns for international super brands. Justin is at the cutting-edge of cool.

Kate Halfpenny
Fashion Designer & Stylist
@Halfpennylondon

Celebrity stylist and fashion designer, Kate is famed for her bespoke creations worn by amazing women such as Rihanna, Erin O'Connor and Kate Moss. She creates costumes for brands such as Hugo Boss, PlayStation and L'Oréal. Her first bridal boutique opened in Bloomsbury in 2013 with her entirely British made collection. Halfpenny London is no longer an industry secret.

Kelly Hoppen MBE
Designer, Author & Entrepreneur
@IMKellyHoppen

A globally renowned designer, Kelly has one of the most celebrated careers in the creative industry. The recipient of numerous awards including an MBE for services to interior design, she is ambassador for the Prince's Trust and the Government's GREAT Campaign. Her studio currently runs over 50 projects and she recently launched an online store, kellyhoppen.com.

'Cool in 2014 is much more individual, niche, and effortless.'
Justin Wilkes

Labrinth
Singer-Songwriter
@Labrinthda1st

Laura Jackson
TV Presenter
@Laura__Jackson

Laura Mvula
Singer-Songwriter
@lauramvula

The artist who has re-imagined the perimeters of pop music's soundscape, Labrinth has more than five million sales to his name since releasing Let the Sun Shine in 2010. His debut album, Electronic Earth, hit number two in the UK album charts. He has also picked up an Ivor Novello, a MOBO award and a BRIT nomination.

Having started her career on T4's music show Freshly Squeezed, Laura is one of TV's brightest rising stars, with a host of fashion, presenting and interviewing jobs under her belt. She has also presented at numerous music festivals and on hit music TV shows.

Signed to RCA, Laura is a unique collision of her Caribbean background and classical music. She has a multitude of nominations and a Top 10 UK album, critically acclaimed Sing To The Moon, to her name. Laura won Best Female and Best RNB/Soul Act at the 2013 MOBO Awards and was one of Britain's Leading Ladies for the AW13 Marks & Spencer campaign.

'Cool is entirely subjective and transient but for me it's things that give me and those around me a feel good factor.'
Laura Mvula

Liz Matthews
Publicist
@lizmatthewspr

Mark Krendel
Managing Director, 8lbs
@mark8lbs

Melissa Odabash
Fashion Designer
@melissaodabash

An entertainment publicist with more than a decade of experience, Liz's client list includes Alexa Chung, Rosie Huntington-Whiteley, Sophie Dahl and Karen Elson. LMPR brands launched in 2013 and accounts include Aspinal of London, Creme de la Mer and Caramel Baby & Child.

Mark has more than a decade of experience structuring commercial opportunities within the music industry. Having established the partnerships division at Universal Music he founded entertainment partnerships specialist 8lbs in 2012. Mark's growing team has delivered campaigns for the likes of boohoo, HSBC and Sony Xperia.

Launched in 1999, Melissa's first swimwear collection swiftly came to epitomize the glamour of a luxury lifestyle brand. Her many partnerships include working with Julien Macdonald for Odabash & Macdonald, and Gwyneth Paltrow for her lifestyle website, GOOP. Melissa also refashioned iconic swimsuits for the films Diana and Imposssible, and has collaborated with Speedo and Bryan Adams.

Millie Kendall MBE
Beauty Brand Creator
@MillieKendall

Natasha McNamara
Digital Editor, glamour.com
@shadyalabama

Phil Clifton
XFM DJ & Presenter
@philclifton

Alongside Anna-Marie Solowij, Millie is Co-Founder of BeautyMART, a disruptive retail concept for beauty at Harvey Nichols, Shoreditch and Topshop and online at thisisbeautymart.com. Millie has been instrumental in the success of many cult beauty brands, from Shu Uemura and Aveda to Ruby & Millie and Concoction Haircare.

Working across lifestyle and fashion websites since 2006, Natasha is Digital Editor of glamour.com, where she oversees the creative direction of the fashion, beauty and celebrity editorial. She is also Editorial Director of easyliving.co.uk, for which she won Launch of the Year 2012 at the British Society of Magazine Editors Awards.

A British television and Sony-nominated radio presenter, Phil currently DJ's for indie and alternative radio station XFM. He also works as a presenter, hosting shows for MTV, Gonzo, Channel 4's flagship music-based breakfast show, Freshly Squeezed, the BRIT Awards 2012, Channel 5, and many more.

2014/15
CoolBrands.uk.com

Reverend and The Makers
Indie-Pop Band
@Reverend_Makers

Ruby Hammer MBE
Make-Up Artist
@RubyMakeup

Sadie Frost
Actress & Fashion Designer
@Sadieliza

At the forefront of the Sheffield scene, Reverend and The Makers released their debut album, The State of Things, in 2007. Their 2009 follow-up, A French Kiss in the Chaos, resulted in a tour with Kasabian and The Enemy. Alongside their Soundsystem club nights, the band's third album, @Reverend Makers, launched in 2012. Their new album, ThirtyTwo, constitutes a resplendent follow-up.

Having had a pioneering influence on the fashion and beauty industries for more than 25 years, Ruby is one of the most respected make-up artists in the world. She has created and been involved with a whole host of cool brands, from Aveda and TweezerMan to Ruby & Millie, and has recently launched her digital platform, rubyhammer.com.

Floozie by Frostfrench and Iris & Edie are Sadie's hugely successful clothing ranges, and Frostfrench will launch a new women's clothing range in 2015. Having produced a feature film, Buttercup Bill, and a short film, Dotty, Sadie is in pre-production for her film Set the Thames on Fire with her production company, Blonde to Black Pictures.

'I think a cool brand is one that crosses boundaries and doesn't pigeonhole people.' **Millie Kendall MBE**

Sam Hall (Goldierocks)
International DJ & Broadcaster
@Goldierocks

Sophie Dahl
International Model & Writer
@sophiedahl

Spark
Singer-Songwriter
@sparkthemusic

The host of a weekly global radio show, The Selector, Sam Hall aka Goldierocks can be heard in over 40 countries worldwide with an audience of over 4.3 million weekly listeners. She routinely performs on the main stages of the world's most popular festivals, as well as travelling the world for philanthropic work with a range of charities.

As well as gracing the cover of Vogue six times, Sophie has modelled in campaigns for the likes of Versace, Alexander McQueen and Yves Saint Laurent. She has published a number of books, including a novel as well as cook books, and launched her website, sophiedahl.com – part journalism and recipe archive, part online magazine – in 2014.

Spark is releasing her music on her own terms. Her new material contains classics by the bucket load; her incredible voice soars through R&B-tinged hits, with catchy melodies to kill for. She's fought hard to get here and now there is everything to play for.

'Cool to me is about innovation. Not being afraid to experiment; to get things wrong in order to get them right and ultimately to create something unique.' **Sam Hall**

Susan Riley
Deputy Editor,
Stylist Magazine
@Susestylist

Tom Findlay
DJ & Producer
@GrooveArmada

Will Best
TV Presenter
@iamwillbest

Having spent more than a decade in the women's and lifestyle publishing sectors, Susan has been Deputy Editor – and twice Acting Editor – of multi-award winning Stylist magazine since its launch in 2009. As part of Shortlist Media Limited's senior editorial team, she's also worked on the development of Stylist France and digital fashion glossy, Never Underdressed.

Tom made his name as one half of the dance music act Groove Armada. Established in 1997, the band has six studio albums and numerous BRIT and Grammy nominations to their name. They founded London's Lovebox festival a decade ago, exiting the business in 2013. Tom lives in London, DJs and continues to produce for the likes of Moda, Hypercolour and Get Physical.

With a contagious passion for all things music, comedy and youth culture, Will is one of the freshest faces in presenting. He was the latest addition to the T4 family when he joined in 2011, presenting alongside Matt Edmondson and Jameela Jamil, and currently hosts Simon Cowell's latest global talent show, You Generation, on YouTube.

Qualifying CoolBrands® 2014/15

- & Other Stories
- 1936 Bière
- 20 Fenchurch Street Sky Garden
- Abel & Cole
- ABSOLUT VODKA
- Absolute Radio
- Ace Hotel
- Acqua Di Parma
- Acqua Panna
- adidas
- adidas miCoach
- Adnams
- Aēsop
- Affordable Art Fair
- AGA
- Agent Provocateur
- Airbnb
- Albion
- Alessi
- Alexander McQueen
- Alexander Wang
- All Star Lanes
- AllSaints
- Alternative Flooring
- American Apparel
- Angostura
- Antonio Federici
- Anya Hindmarch
- Apple
- Artisan du Chocolat
- Asahi
- Ascaso
- Asics
- ASOS
- Aspall Cyder
- Asprey
- Aston Manor
- Aston Martin
- Audi
- Aveda
- Badoit
- Balthazar
- Bang & Olufsen
- bareMinerals
- Barker and Stonehouse
- Baskin Robbins
- BBC
- BBC iPlayer
- BEAR
- Beats by Dr. Dre
- Belu Water
- Belvedere Vodka
- Belvoir Fruit Farms
- Ben & Jerry's
- Benefit
- Bentley
- Berghaus
- Bestival
- Beyond Dark
- Bicester Village
- Bill's
- Biona
- Bisque
- Björn Borg
- Black Dragon
- Blakes London
- Blaupunkt
- BMW
- Bobbi Brown
- Bocca di Lupo
- BoConcept
- BODIE and FOU
- Boffi
- Bolin Webb
- Bollinger
- Bombay Sapphire
- Bootcamp Pilates
- Borough Market
- Bose
- Bottlegreen
- Bounce Energy Balls
- Bowers & Wilkins
- BOXPARK
- BrewDog
- British Airways
- Brylcreem
- BULLDOG
- Bullring Birmingham
- Bulthaup
- Bumble and bumble
- Burberry
- Burger & Lobster
- Burts Potato Chips
- Byron
- C.P. Hart
- Cabot Circus
- Café Direct
- Cambridge Audio
- Cambridge Satchel Company
- Camden Town Brewery
- Canard-Duchêne
- Canon
- Capital FM
- Carnaby
- Champagne Perrier-Jouët
- CHANEL
- Channel 4
- Chapel Down
- Charbonnel et Walker
- Charles Worthington
- Charlotte Olympia
- Chi
- Chloé
- Chococo
- Christian Louboutin
- Church's
- Ciaté
- Clarins
- Clarisonic
- Clipper
- Cobra
- Coco de Mer
- Cocoa Deli
- Cocoa Runners
- Cole & Mason
- Conscious Chocolate
- Converse All Stars
- COS
- Courvoisier
- Covent Garden
- Crème de la Mer
- Crussh
- Curzon Cinemas
- D.L. & Co.
- Dabbous
- Daunt Books
- Daylesford
- Deezer
- De'Longhi
- Dermalogica
- Destinology
- Dinner by Heston Blumenthal
- Dior
- Diptyque
- Dirty Pretty Things
- Dolce & Gabbana
- Dom Pérignon
- Dover Street Market
- Dr Sebagh
- Dr Stuart's
- Dr. Martens
- Dr.Hauschka
- Dragonfly Tea
- Duck & Waffle
- Duvel
- EA
- Eden Project
- Edie Parker
- Edinburgh International Festival
- Elite London
- Ella's Kitchen
- EMI
- English Cheesecake Company
- Estrella Damm
- Etsy
- EVE LOM
- Everyman Cinemas
- Evian
- Eyeko
- Facebook
- Farrow & Ball
- Feel Good Drinks Co
- Fendi
- Fentimans
- Ferrari
- Festival No.6
- Fever-Tree
- Fired Earth
- Firefly Tonics
- first direct
- Fisher & Paykel
- Five Guys
- Fleur of England
- Foyles
- Frame
- Fred & Ginger
- Freya
- Frieze Art Fair
- Frostfrench
- Fudges
- Gaggenau
- Gaggia
- GAIL'S
- Gaucho
- ghd
- Givenchy
- Glastonbury
- G'NOSH
- Google
- GoPro
- Graham & Brown
- Grain Store
- graze.com
- Great British Sauce Company
- Green & Black's Organic
- Green Man Festival
- Gressingham Duck
- Grey Goose
- Grove Organic Fruit Co.
- Gü
- Guinness
- GYMBOX
- H&M
- Häagen-Dazs
- Hampstead Tea
- Harley-Davidson
- Harman Kardon
- Harrogate Spring Water
- Hatterrall Ridge
- Havaianas
- Hawksmoor
- Heal's
- Hendrick's Gin
- Hennessy
- Hershesons
- HILLIER
- HIP Hotels
- Hix
- Home House
- Honest Burgers
- Honeyrose Bakery
- Hotel Café Royal
- Hotel Chocolat
- Hotel du Vin
- House Envy
- House of Dorchester
- House of Hackney
- HouseTrip
- hülsta
- Hummus Bros
- Hunter
- Illamasqua
- IMG Models
- Independent
- Innocent
- Instagram
- Isle of Wight Festival
- itsu
- ITV
- Jack Daniel's
- Jaguar
- James Brown London
- Jameson
- Jamie Oliver (Products)
- Jawbone
- JBL
- Jelly Belly
- Jimmy Choo
- Jimmy's Iced Coffee
- JO LOVES
- Jo Malone
- Joe & Seph's
- John Frieda
- John Lewis
- Johnnie Walker
- Joseph Joseph
- Jude's
- Juniper Green Organic Gin
- Jura
- Kérastase
- KETTLE Chips
- Kiehl's
- Kindle

2014/15
CoolBrands.uk.com

- Kirin Ichiban
- Kiss
- KitchenAid
- Klipsch
- Konami
- Konditor & Cook
- Kopparberg
- Korres
- Krispy Kreme
- Krug
- La Perla
- Lady Dinah's Cat Emporium
- Lamborghini
- Laphroaig
- L'Artisan Parfumeur
- Last.fm
- Latitude
- Laura Mercier
- Laurent-Perrier
- Lavazza
- Le Creuset
- Le Gavroche
- Le Manoir aux Quat'Saisons
- Le Pain Quotidien
- Leatherman
- Leica
- Leon
- Levi's
- LG
- Liberty
- Ligne Roset
- Lilou et Loïc
- Linda Farrow
- Lindt
- Linn
- Little Greene
- Liz Earle
- L'OCCITANE
- Loewe
- London Designer Outlet
- London Fields Brewery
- Louis Roederer
- Løv Organic
- LSA International
- Luscombe
- LUXE City Guides
- M.A.C
- Made.com
- Magimix
- Maker's Mark
- Malmaison
- Manolo Blahnik
- Marc Jacobs
- Marmite
- Marshfield Farm Ice Cream
- Maserati
- MATCHESFASHION.COM
- MAWI
- McLaren Automotive
- ME London
- Mercedes-Benz
- Mercier
- Michael Aram
- Miele
- Milk & Honey
- Miller Harris
- MINI
- Minx Nails
- Models 1
- Moët & Chandon
- Moleskine
- Monkey Shoulder
- Monmouth
- Moroccanoil
- Mövenpick Ice Cream
- Mr & Mrs Smith
- Mr Organic
- MR PORTER
- MTV
- Mulberry
- Mungo & Maud
- Myla
- nails inc.
- Näkd.
- Naked Wines
- NARS
- Neal's Yard Remedies
- Neom Organics
- Nespresso
- NET-A-PORTER
- Netflix
- New Balance
- Nicolas Kirkwood
- Nike
- Nike+ FuelBand
- Nikon
- Nintendo
- No 5 Cavendish Sq.
- No.1 Lounges
- Nokia
- notonthehighstreet.com
- Nyetimber
- O2 Academy
- Office
- Old Jamaica Ginger Beer
- OLEHENRIKSEN
- Oliver Bonas
- Olympus
- onefinestay
- OPI
- Orchard Pig
- Orla Kiely
- Ottolenghi
- Oxford Covered Market
- Paperchase
- Patagonia
- Patrón Tequila
- Paul
- Paul Mitchell
- Pedlars
- Penhaligon's
- Percy & Reed
- Peroni Nastro Azzurro
- Perrier
- Peyton and Byrne
- Philip Kingsley
- Picturehouse Cinemas
- Pimm's
- Pinkberry
- Pinterest
- Pipers
- Pizza East
- PlayStation
- Plymouth Gin
- Poggenpohl
- Pollen Street Social
- popchips
- Porsche
- Portobello Road Market
- Prada
- Premier Model Management
- Prestat
- Pret A Manger
- Pretty Polly
- PROPERCORN
- Pukka
- Puma
- Punchdrunk
- Quintessentially Group
- Rapha
- Rare Tea Company
- Raw Health
- Ray-Ban
- Red Carpet Manicure
- Reebok
- Reiss
- Rekorderlig
- Rémy Martin
- Restaurant Gordon Ramsey
- Riedel
- Rigby & Peller
- Riverford
- Rockett St George
- Rockstar Games
- Rococo Chocolates
- Rodial
- Rolex
- Rolls-Royce
- Roundhouse
- Royal Albert Hall
- Ruinart
- Rupert Sanderson
- Russian Standard Vodka
- S.Pellegrino
- Salty Dog
- Samsung
- San Miguel
- Sanderson
- Sandford Orchards
- Sauza Tequila
- SB.TV
- Seabrook Crisps
- Searcys | The Gherkin
- Seche
- Secret Cinema
- Secret Escapes
- Secret Garden Party
- SEGA
- Select Model Management
- Selfridges
- Sennheiser
- Seven Dials
- Shake Shack
- Shazam
- Shiseido
- simplehuman
- Sipsmith
- Sisley
- SkinCeuticals
- Skullcandy
- Sky Atlantic
- Skype
- Smeg
- Snog
- Snow+Rock
- Soap & Glory
- SodaStream
- Soho House Group
- Sonos
- Sony
- Sony Music
- Sophia Webster
- Soundcloud
- Southbank Centre
- Space.NK
- Specialized
- Speyside Glenlivet
- Spitalfields
- Spotify
- Spotted by Locals
- Square Pie
- St Martins Lane
- St. Tropez
- Stella McCartney
- Stephen Webster
- Sticks'n'Sushi
- Storm
- Story
- Sweaty Betty
- T&G
- TAG Heuer
- Taittinger
- Tangle Teezer
- Tanqueray
- Tassimo
- Taste of London
- Tea Palace
- teapigs
- The Artisan Kitchen
- The Arts Club
- The Berry Company
- The Breakfast Club
- The Brompton Club
- The Clove Club
- The Club at the Ivy
- The Collective Dairy
- The Connaught
- The Co-operative Bank
- The Cornish Crisp Company
- The Dormen
- The Fat Duck
- The French Bedroom Company
- The French House
- The Garrick Club
- The Glenlivet
- The Great Escape
- The Hand and Flowers
- The Herdy Company
- The Hospital Club
- The House of St. Barnabas
- The Kernel
- The Ledbury
- Echo Arena Liverpool
- The London EDITION
- The London Tea Company
- The Lowry Hotel
- The Macallan
- The May Fair
- The New Craftsmen
- The North Face
- The O2
- The Original Candy Company
- The Rookery
- The Saucy Fish Co.
- The Third Space
- The View From The Shard
- The White Company
- The Zetter Townhouse
- Tiffany & Co.
- Tiger Beer
- TIGI
- Tom Dixon
- Tom Ford
- TONI&GUY
- Topshop
- Tossed
- Town Hall Hotel
- Trinity Leeds
- triyoga
- True Grace
- Tumblr
- Tunetribe
- Twinings
- Twitter
- Ty Nant
- Tyrrells
- Ubisoft
- Ubuntu
- Uniqlo
- Universal Music
- Urban Decay
- Urban Fruit
- Urban Outfitters
- URBANARA
- Urbanears
- Vans
- Vespa
- Veuve Clicquot
- VEVO
- Victoria's Secret
- Villeroy & Boch
- Vimeo
- Virgin Atlantic
- Virgin Money
- Vita Coco
- Vitamix
- Vitra
- Vivienne Westwood
- VOSS
- Wagamama
- WAH Nails
- Warner Music
- Westfield
- Whole Foods
- Wilderness
- William Morris Endeavor
- Willie's Cacao
- Wolford
- Wonderbra
- Xbox
- yoomoo
- YouTube
- YSL
- Zara
- ZICO
- Zipcar
- Zumba

Please note that some brand names have been changed since the research was conducted. This list reflects the brands as they are generally marketed at the time of going to press and may differ slightly from the name analysed in the survey.